GCSE Biology

Set A Paper 1

Higher Tier

In addition to this paper you should have:
• A ruler.
• A calculator.

Centre name				
Centre number				
Candidate number				

Surname	
Other names	
Candidate signature	

Time allowed:
• 1 hour 45 minutes

Instructions to candidates
• Write your name and other details in the spaces provided above.
• Answer **all** questions in the spaces provided.
• Do all rough work on the paper.
• Cross out any work you do not want to be marked.

Information for candidates
• The marks available are given in brackets at the end of each question.
• There are 100 marks available for this paper.
• You are allowed to use a calculator.
• You should use good English and present your answers in a clear and organised way.

Advice to candidates
• In calculations show clearly how you worked out your answers.

	For examiner's use					
Q	\multicolumn{3}{c}{Attempt Nº}	Q	\multicolumn{3}{c}{Attempt Nº}
	1	2	3		1	2	3
1				6			
2				7			
3				8			
4				9			
5				10			
			Total			

Answer **all** questions in the spaces provided

1 *Salmonella* is a type of bacteria which causes disease in humans.

1.1 Which of the following infectious diseases is also caused by bacteria?
Tick **one** box.

☐ Measles

☐ Gonorrhoea

☐ Malaria

☐ HIV

[1 mark]

1.2 Give **two** symptoms of *Salmonella* food poisoning.

1. ....

2. ....
[2 marks]

1.3 Compare how bacteria and viruses cause symptoms in a host.

....

....

....
[2 marks]

Figure 1 shows a diagram of a *Salmonella* bacterium.

Figure 1

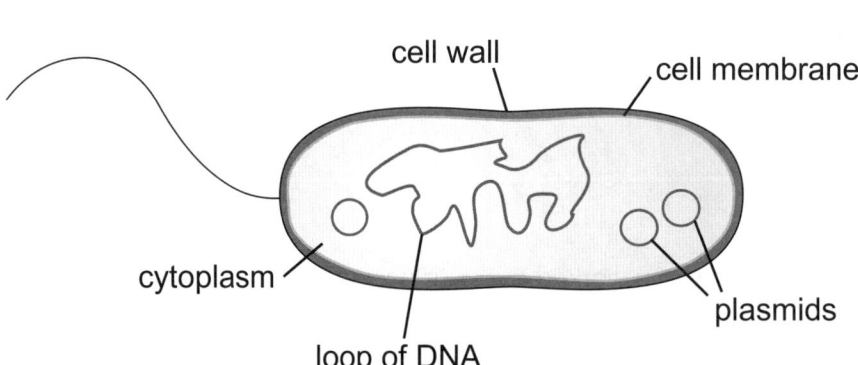

1.4 Give **two** features of the bacterium in **Figure 1** which show that *Salmonella* is a prokaryote and not a eukaryote.

1. ....

2. ....
[2 marks]

1.5 An electron microscope image is produced of a *Salmonella* bacterium.

- The length of the bacterium in the image is 18 millimetres (mm).
- The real length of the bacterium is 4 micrometres (μm).

Calculate the magnification of the image.
Use the equation:

$$\text{magnification} = \frac{\text{image size}}{\text{real size}}$$

magnification = × ....
[2 marks]

1.6 *Salmonella* bacteria can enter a person's body via contaminated food.
They cause illness when they reach the cells of the intestines.
Explain how the human body defends itself against infection by *Salmonella* once the pathogen has been ingested.

....

....

....

....

....

....
[4 marks]

Turn over for the next question

Turn over ▶

2 Some pondweed was used to investigate how the amount of light available affects the rate of photosynthesis.

The apparatus that was used for this experiment is shown in **Figure 2**.

Figure 2

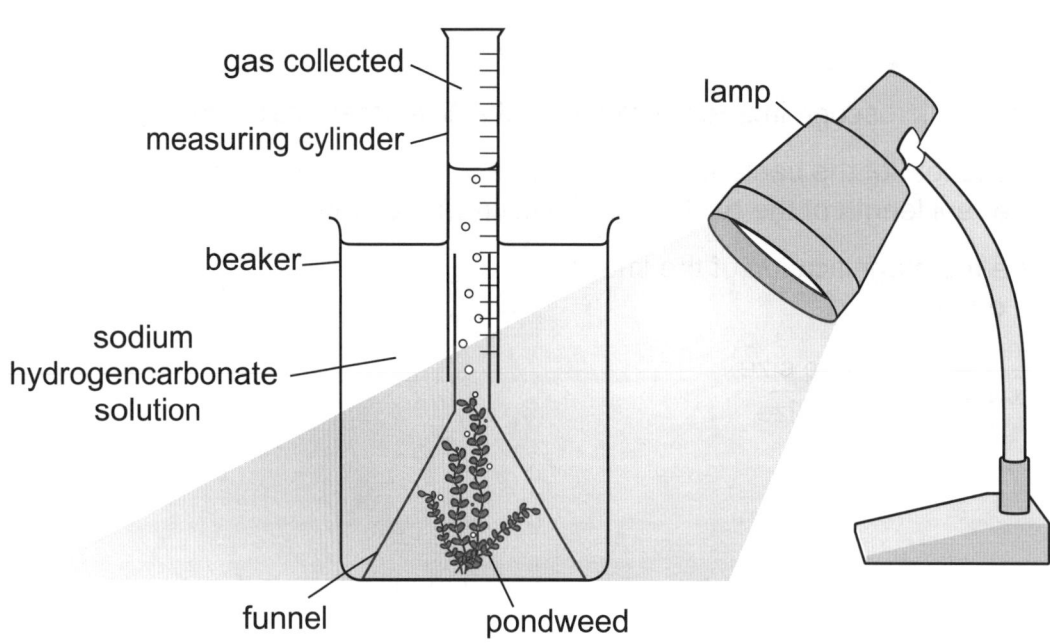

2.1 What gas is being collected in the measuring cylinder?

....

[1 mark]

2.2 What would happen to the volume of gas collected if the investigation was repeated with the lamp turned off? Give a reason for your answer.

....

....

....

....

[3 marks]

4

2.3 Sodium hydrogencarbonate dissolves in water and releases carbon dioxide.
Suggest why sodium hydrogencarbonate was added to the water in this experiment.

....

....

....

[2 marks]

Table 1 shows the volume of gas collected in the measuring cylinder over 1 hour.

Table 1

Time (min)	10	20	30	40	50	60
Total volume of gas collected (cm³)	1.0	3.0	6.0	7.0	7.5	8.0

2.4 Use data from **Table 1** to calculate the mean rate of photosynthesis over 1 hour.
Give your answer in cm³/min.
Give your answer to 2 significant figures.

Rate of photosynthesis = ... cm³/min

[2 marks]

2.5 The temperature of the sodium hydrogencarbonate solution was discovered to have increased slightly during the investigation.
Explain why this might have affected the rate of photosynthesis of the pondweed.

....

....

[1 mark]

2.6 Suggest how temperature could have been controlled in the experiment.

....

....

[1 mark]

Question 2 continues on the next page

Turn over ▶

2.7 The investigation could have been conducted by counting the number of bubbles given off in a certain amount of time by the pondweed.
Suggest **one** advantage of using a measuring cylinder rather than counting bubbles.

....

....
[1 mark]

2.8 When plants photosynthesise they produce glucose.
Give **three** ways plants use the glucose they produce.

1. ....

2. ....

3. ....
[3 marks]

3 This question is about the digestive system.

3.1 Describe how starch is broken down in the mouth and small intestine.

....

....

....

[2 marks]

A sample of food contains starch. The sample is crushed and put into a test tube. A solution containing enzymes is added to the test tube.

3.2 Describe a test that could be used to determine whether or not the starch in the sample has been broken down by the enzymes.

....

....

....

[2 marks]

3.3 Bile is a digestive fluid stored in the gall bladder.
Which of the following organs produces bile?
Tick **one** box.

☐ Liver

☐ Stomach

☐ Small intestine

☐ Gall bladder

[1 mark]

Question 3 continues on the next page

Turn over ▶

Gallstones are small, solid stones formed mainly of excess cholesterol. They can block the bile ducts (tubes) that connect the gall bladder to the small intestine.

3.4 Explain why eating fatty foods might cause a problem for people suffering from gallstones.

....

....

....

....

....

[4 marks]

blankLeav
blan

8

© CGP 2017 — copying more than
5% of this paper is not permitted

4 **Figure 3** shows some molecules moving through a cell membrane.

Figure 3

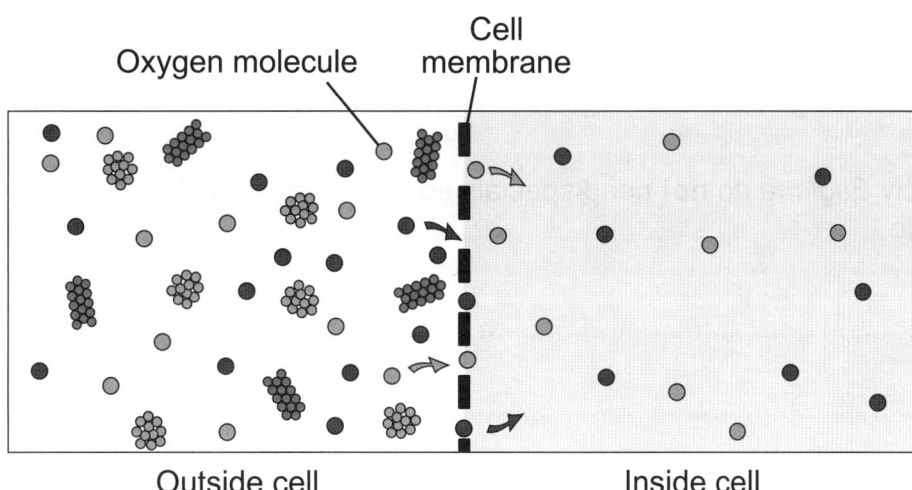

4.1 Describe the process by which oxygen moves into cells.

....

....

....

....

[3 marks]

4.2 The rate of aerobic respiration increases inside the cell in **Figure 3**.
Explain what will happen to the rate of oxygen movement across the cell membrane.

....

....

....

....

[3 marks]

Question 4 continues on the next page

Turn over ▶

Trout are freshwater fish. They are relatively large, multicellular organisms with specialised exchange organs.

Euglena are small, single-celled organisms that live in water. They do not have specialised exchange organs.

Both trout and *Euglena* need oxygen to survive.

4.3 Explain why *Euglena* do **not** need specialised organs for absorbing oxygen, but trout do.

....

....

....

....

....

....

....

[4 marks]

5   **Figure 4** shows how the concentration of lactic acid in a cyclist's blood changes with different work rates.

Figure 4

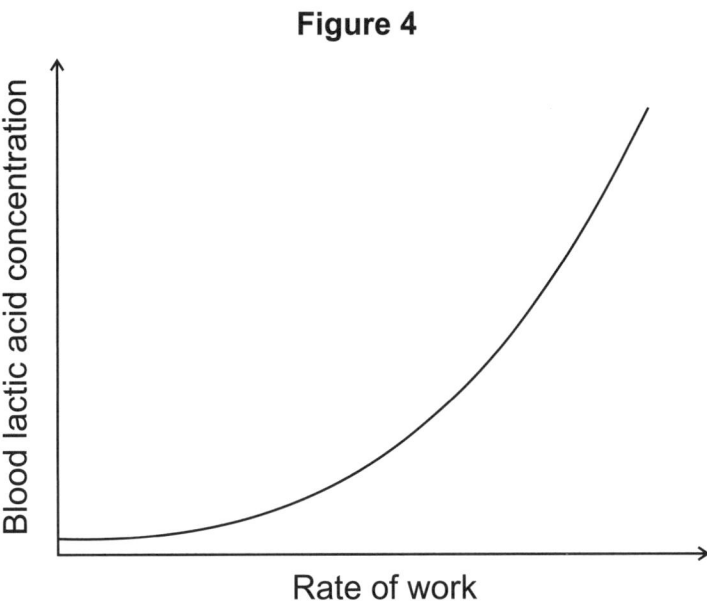

5.1   Describe the trend shown by **Figure 4**.

....

....

....

[2 marks]

5.2   Suggest a reason for the trend you have described above.

....

....

....

....

....

[3 marks]

Question 5 continues on the next page

Turn over ▶

5.3 The cyclist takes part in a sprint race.
Explain what will happen to the cyclist's pulse rate and breathing rate immediately after her race.

....12...

....

....

....

....

[3 marks]

5.4 The cyclist rests after the sprint race.
Describe how the cyclist's heart rate is controlled at rest.

....

....

[1 mark]

6   Tobacco smoke contains chemicals that can cause malignant tumours.

6.1   Describe why malignant tumours are cancerous but benign tumours are not.

....

....

....

[2 marks]

A study compared the incidence of cancer per 100 000 men and the number of cigarettes they smoke per day. The results are shown in **Table 2**.

Table 2

Number of cigarettes smoked per day	Incidence of cancer per 100 000 men
10	50
20	120
30	230
40	420

6.2   Complete **Figure 5** using the data from **Table 2**.

- Complete the *y*-axis. Include a label and use a suitable scale.
- Plot the incidence of cancer per 100 000 men.
- Draw a curve of best fit.

Figure 5

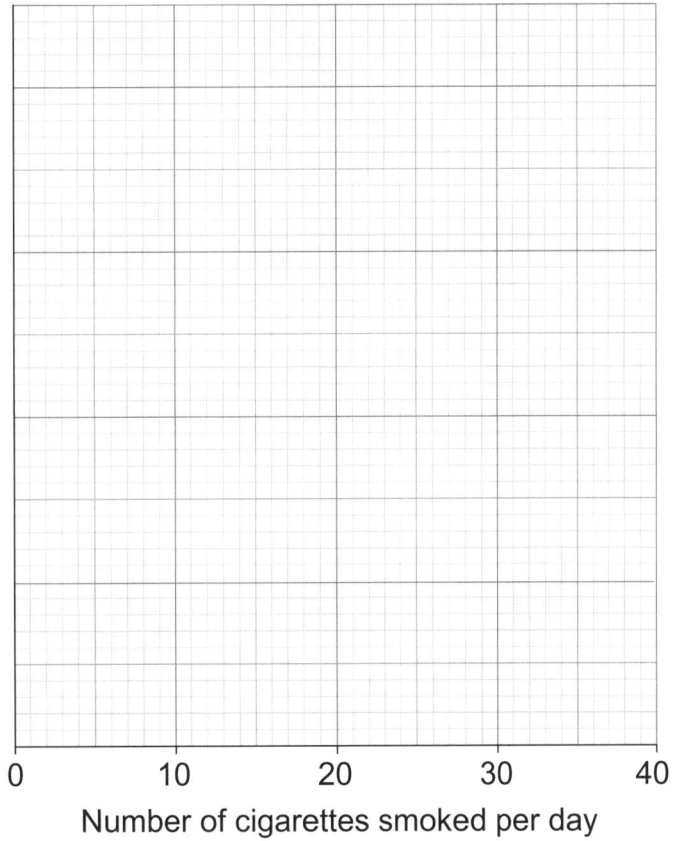

Number of cigarettes smoked per day

[3 marks]

Question 6 continues on the next page

Turn over ▶

6.3   A scientific magazine used the data in **Table 2** to report that people who smoke are more likely to die from cancer than people who don't smoke.
Does the data support this conclusion? Give reasons for your answer.

....14...

....

....

....

[3 marks]

14

7 Two students carried out an experiment to investigate the effects of different minerals on plant growth. Their teacher gave them three pea plants of the same species, all of a similar height. The method they used is described below.

1. Measure the height of the three pea plants.

2. Add a solution containing minerals to three beakers as follows:

   • Beaker A: solution high in magnesium and nitrates.
   • Beaker B: solution high in magnesium and low in nitrates.
   • Beaker C: solution low in magnesium and high in nitrates.

3. Place a pea plant in each of the beakers, **A**, **B** and **C**.

4. Leave the plants to grow for one week.

5. Measure the height of each of the plants at the end of the week.

The results of the students' experiment are shown in **Table 3**.

Table 3

Beaker	Height at start (cm)	Height at end (cm)	Percentage change in height (%)
A	4	9	125
B	5	7	40
C	4	7	

7.1 Calculate the percentage change in height for the plant in Beaker **C**.

....%
[2 marks]

7.2 Explain why the growth in Beaker **B** was poor.

....

....

....

[3 marks]

Question 7 continues on the next page

Turn over ▶

7.3 Describe how you would expect the pea plant in Beaker **C**, which was low in magnesium, to look at the end of the week. Explain your answer.

....

....
[2 marks]

7.4 State **two** variables that the students would have had to control for each beaker.

1. ....

2. ....
[2 marks]

7.5 Aside from controlling variables, give **one** way in which the students could have improved their method in order to obtain more valid results.

....

....
[1 mark]

7.6 Give **one** conclusion you can draw from this experiment.

....

....
[1 mark]

8 **Figure 6** shows a cell, labelled **Y**, in one of the stages of mitosis.

Figure 6

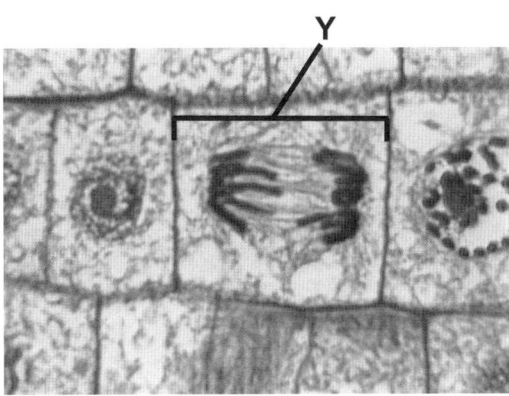

8.1 Describe what needs to happen to a cell before mitosis can begin.

....

....

....

[2 marks]

8.2 Describe what will happen next to the cell labelled **Y** in **Figure 6**.

....

....

....

[2 marks]

8.3 A scientist collects 20 cells from a sample.
The cells divide by mitosis once every 20 minutes.
Estimate how many cells will be in the sample after 2 hours.
Give your answer in standard form.

number of cells = ...

[3 marks]

Question 8 continues on the next page

Turn over ▶

Figure 7 shows part of a eukaryotic organism's life cycle.

Figure 7

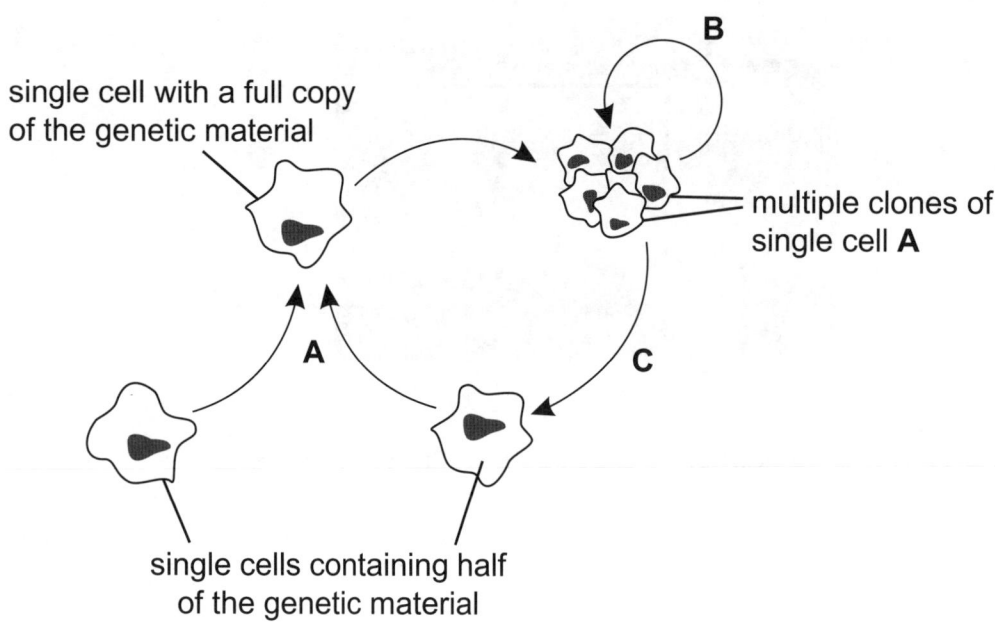

single cell with a full copy
of the genetic material

B

multiple clones of
single cell **A**

A

C

single cells containing half
of the genetic material

8.4 Which of the stages, **A**, **B** or **C**, shown in **Figure 7** involves mitosis?
Give a reason for your answer.

Stage: ....

Reason: ....

....

[2 marks]

9 Read the following information about myeloma.

1. Myeloma is a cancer of the plasma cells — a type of white blood cell.

2. Plasma cells are produced in the bone marrow.

3. Chemotherapy can be used to kill cancerous plasma cells. Chemotherapy is also likely to kill or damage healthy cells in the patient's bone marrow.

4. A bone marrow transplant can be used following chemotherapy to treat myeloma.

9.1 An individual with myeloma is treated with chemotherapy to kill their cancerous plasma cells. Suggest how a bone marrow transplant from a donor may then be used to treat the individual.

....

....

....

....

[2 marks]

Question 9 continues on the next page

Turn over ▶

19

Both adult and embryonic stem cells have the potential to be used for medical treatments.

9.2 Evaluate the potential use of adult and embryonic stem cells as medical treatments. Your answer should include a justified conclusion.

....

....

....

....

....

....

....

....

....

[4 marks]

10 In 1970, a new antibiotic was discovered which was very effective against disease X. Doctors have been prescribing this drug ever since.
Figure 8 shows the number of deaths from disease X over time.

Figure 8

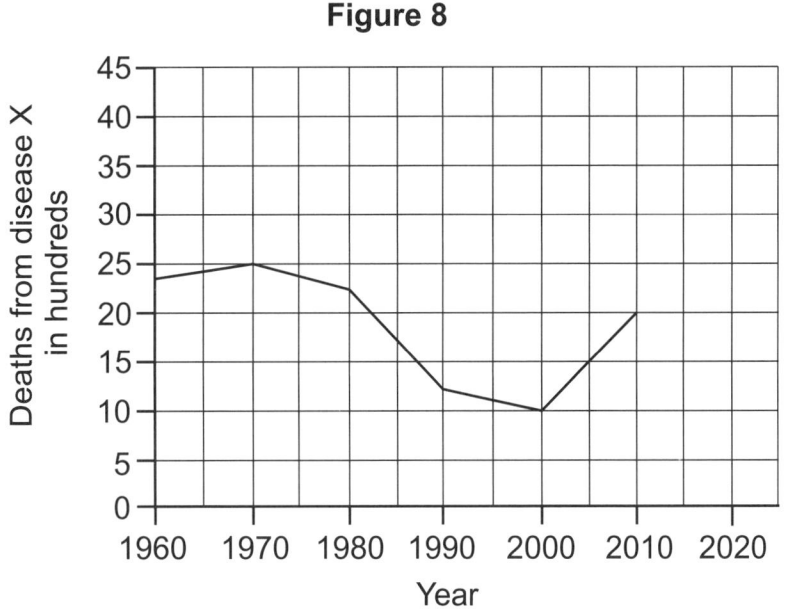

10.1 Between 1970 and 2000, there was an overall decrease in the number of deaths per year from disease X.
Use **Figure 8** to calculate the mean rate at which the number of deaths per year decreased.

Rate of decrease = ... deaths per year
[2 marks]

10.2 Use **Figure 8** to predict the number of deaths from disease X in 2020.
Assume the rate of increase from the year 2000 remains constant.

Predicted number of deaths in 2020 = ...
[1 mark]

Question 10 continues on the next page

Turn over ▶

21

Figure 9 shows two agar plates. Agar plates are Petri dishes containing a culture medium of agar jelly. The bacteria that cause disease X are growing on each plate.

- The first plate shows the results of an experiment carried out in 1975.
- The second plate shows the results when the experiment was repeated in 2005 using a fresh sample of bacteria.

Figure 9

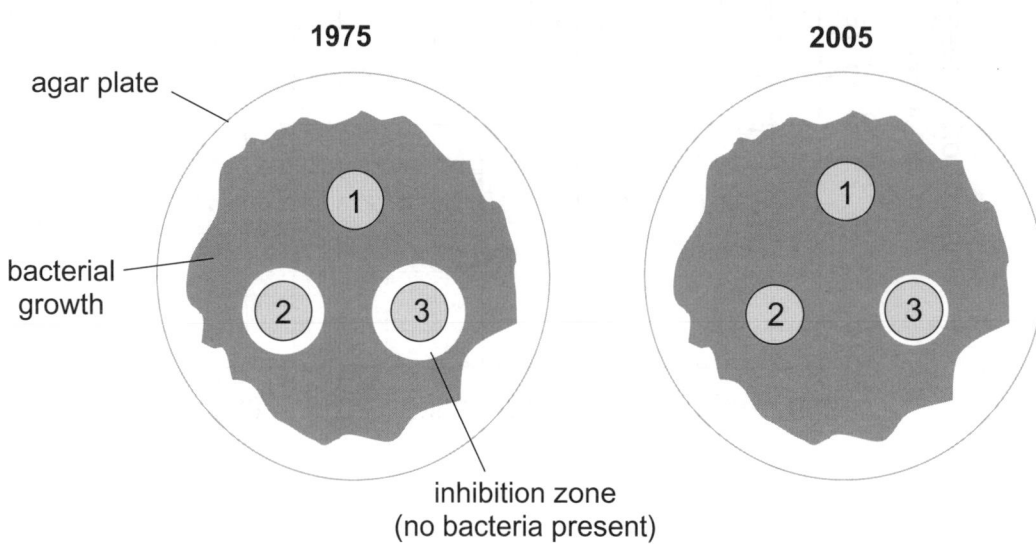

On each plate, there are three paper discs.

- Disc 1 is a control. It is soaked in distilled water only.
- Discs 2 and 3 are soaked in different concentrations of the antibiotic used to treat disease X.

10.3 Give **two** steps that scientists carrying out these experiments should have taken in order to prevent the plates being contaminated with unwanted microorganisms.

1. ....

....

2. ....

....

[2 marks]

10.4 Use the experimental evidence from **Figure 9** to explain the trends shown in the graph in **Figure 8**.

....

....

....

....

....

....

....

....

....

....

[6 marks]

END OF QUESTIONS

GCSE Biology

Set B Paper 1

Higher Tier

In addition to this paper you should have:	**Centre name**
• A ruler.	**Centre number**
• A calculator.	**Candidate number**

Surname
Other names
Candidate signature

Time allowed:
• 1 hour 45 minutes

Instructions to candidates
• Write your name and other details in the spaces provided above.
• Answer **all** questions in the spaces provided.
• Do all rough work on the paper.
• Cross out any work you do not want to be marked.

Information for candidates
• The marks available are given in brackets at the end of each question.
• There are 100 marks available for this paper.
• You are allowed to use a calculator.
• You should use good English and present your answers in a clear and organised way.

Advice to candidates
• In calculations show clearly how you worked out your answers.

For examiner's use

Q	Attempt Nº			Q	Attempt Nº		
	1	2	3		1	2	3
1				5			
2				6			
3				7			
4				8			
Total							

Answer **all** questions in the spaces provided

1   **Figure 1** shows three different types of specialised plant cell.

Figure 1

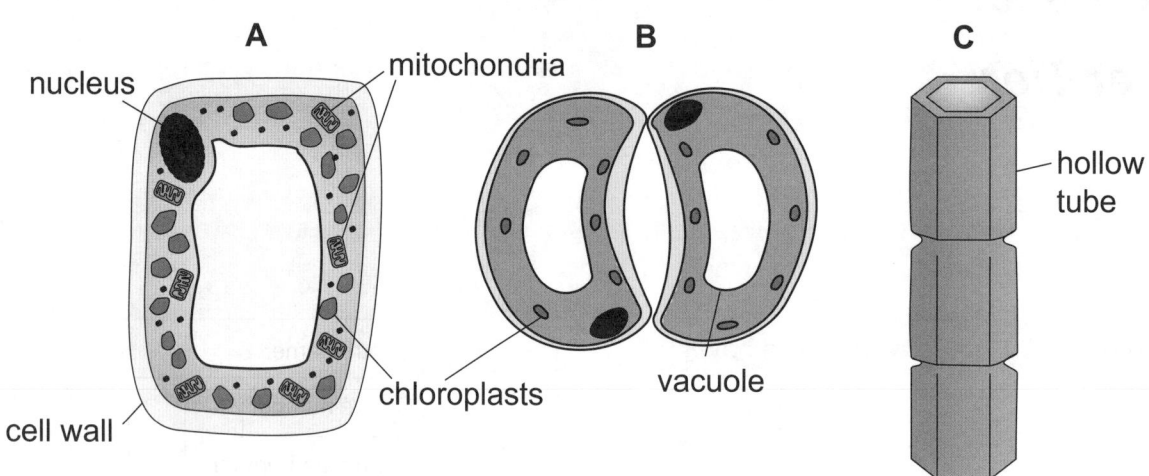

1.1   Which subcellular structure labelled in **Figure 1** contains cellulose?

....

[1 mark]

1.2   Draw **one** line to match each plant cell type in **Figure 1** to the main function that it performs.

Cell   **Function**

A   Carrying water and ions around the plant.

B   Controlling the movement of gases in and out of the plant.

C   Carrying out photosynthesis.

[2 marks]

1.3   The growing tip of a plant shoot contains meristem tissue.
Explain why all the cells in **Figure 1** can be grown from the growing tip of a plant shoot.

....

....

[2 marks]

1.4 A root hair cell is another type of specialised plant cell.
Explain how a root hair cell is adapted to its function.

....

....

....

[3 marks]

1.5 Photosynthesis is an important reaction carried out in certain plant cells.
Which of the following chemical symbols shows a **product** of photosynthesis?
Tick **one** box.

☐ H_2O

☐ CO_2

☐ $C_6H_{12}O_6$

☐ H_2

[1 mark]

Both plant and animal cells contain a nucleus.

1.6 Describe the function of the nucleus in a cell.

....

....

[1 mark]

1.7 Give **three** ways in which animal cells differ from plant cells.

1. ....

2. ....

3. ....

[3 marks]

Turn over for the next question

Turn over ▶

2 Antibiotics are used to treat bacterial diseases.

Leav blan

2.1 Which of the following scientists discovered the antibiotic penicillin? Tick **one** box.

☐ Gregor Mendel

☐ Carl Woese

☐ Charles Darwin

☐ Alexander Fleming

[1 mark]

Figure 2 shows the number of bacteria in a patient's blood during a course of antibiotics.

Figure 2

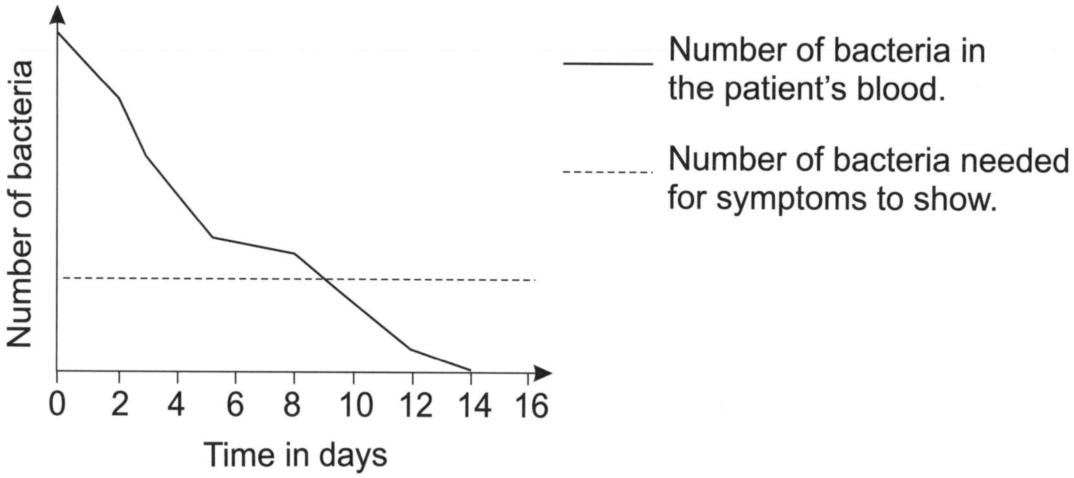

——— Number of bacteria in the patient's blood.

------- Number of bacteria needed for symptoms to show.

2.2 How long after starting the antibiotics did the patient's symptoms disappear?

Time taken for symptoms to disappear = ... days

[1 mark]

2.3 Explain why it is important that the patient was given the right type of antibiotic for his infection.

....

....

[1 mark]

2.4 A wide range of antibiotics are used to treat bacterial infections. Explain why it is harder to develop drugs to treat viruses than to treat bacterial infections.

....

....

....

[2 marks]

© CGP 2017 — copying more than 5% of this paper is not permitted

Figure 3 shows a sample of the patient's blood viewed under a light microscope.

Figure 3

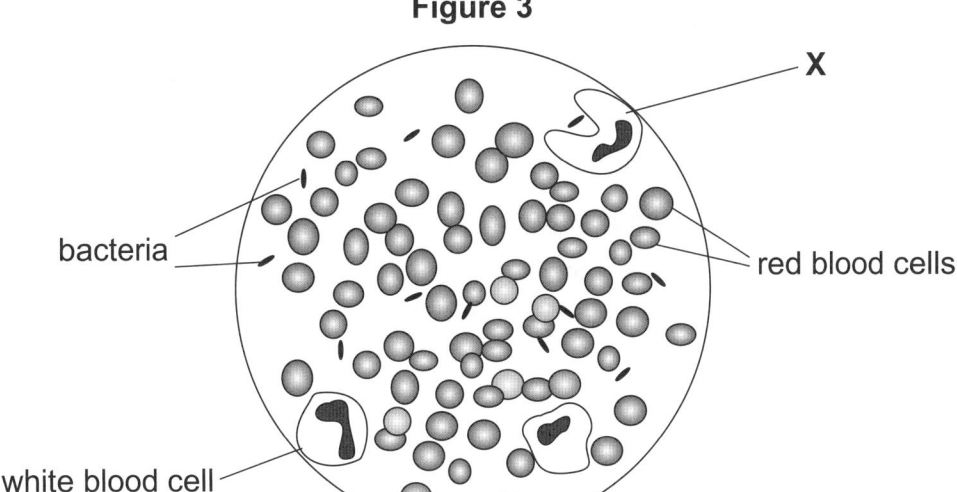

2.5   The white blood cell labelled **X** in **Figure 3** has changed shape to engulf the bacteria.
Which process is cell **X** carrying out?
Tick **one** box.

☐   emulsification

☐   mitosis

☐   phagocytosis

☐   photosynthesis

[1 mark]

2.6   Apart from the process being carried out by cell **X**, give **two** ways that
white blood cells help to defend against pathogens.

1. ....

2. ....
[2 marks]

2.7   The blood sample was viewed with a magnification of × 600.
A scientist measured the image of one of the bacteria to be 3 mm long.
Calculate the actual length of the bacterium that the scientist measured.
Use the equation:

$$\text{magnification} = \frac{\text{size of image}}{\text{size of real object}}$$

actual length of bacterium = ... mm
[2 marks]

Turn over for the next question

Turn over ▶

3   Trypsin is an enzyme that breaks down proteins. A student decided to investigate the effect of pH on trypsin activity. She used milk powder as a source of protein in her experiment. This is the method she used:

1.   She added milk powder to a beaker and mixed it with distilled water to create a milk powder solution. She added a set volume of this solution to six test tubes.

2.   Next, she added a buffer solution with a different pH value to each test tube.

3.   Then, she added a set volume and concentration of trypsin to each tube.

4.   She timed how long it took each solution to turn from cloudy to clear. This change indicated that all of the protein in the milk powder had been broken down.

The results of the experiment are shown in **Table 1**.

Table 1

pH	time taken for reaction (seconds)
5	365
6	280
7	200
8	120
9	245
10	350

3.1   Use data from **Table 1** to draw a graph on **Figure 4**.

- Complete the *y*-axis. Include a label and a suitable scale.
- Plot the time taken for the reaction.
- Join the points with straight lines.

Figure 4

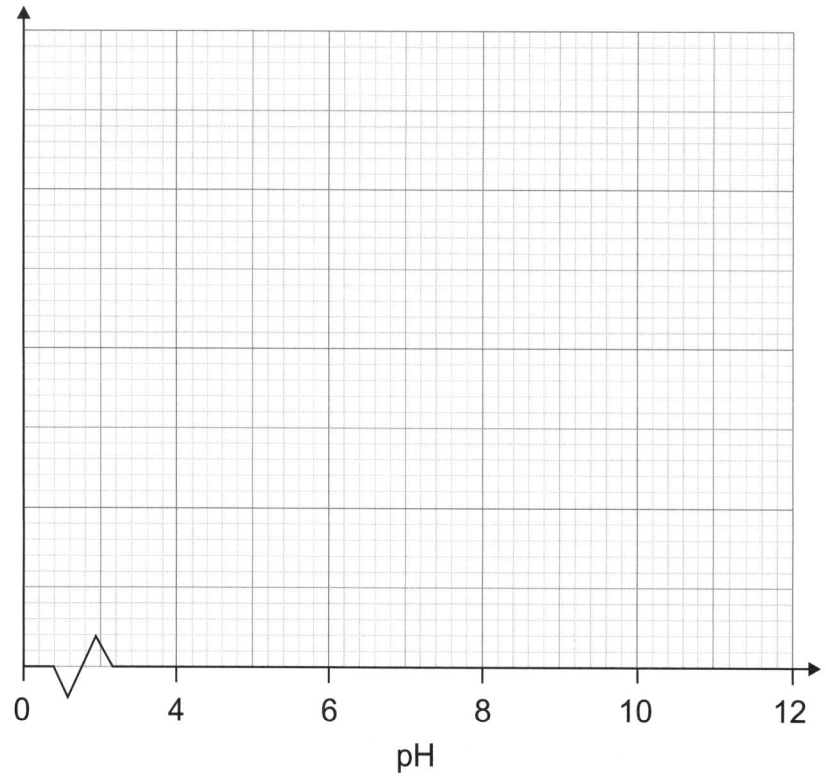

pH

[4 marks]

3.2 Use **Table 1** to estimate the optimum pH for the trypsin.

....
[1 mark]

3.3 Give the dependent and independent variables for this experiment.

Dependent variable: ....

Independent variable: ....
[2 marks]

3.4 Suggest an explanation as to why the reaction is very slow at certain pH levels.

....

....

....

....
[3 marks]

3.5 The student carried all of the experiments out at room temperature.
Explain how using a water bath could have made her results more valid.

....

....

....
[2 marks]

3.6 Trypsin is a protein.
The student adds some biuret solution to one of the test tubes at the end of
the experiment and gently shakes the tube.
What colour will the solution in the test tube be? Give a reason for your answer.

Colour: ....

Reason: ....

....
[2 marks]

Turn over for the next question

Turn over ▶

4   **Figure 5** shows a diagram of the lungs.

Figure 5

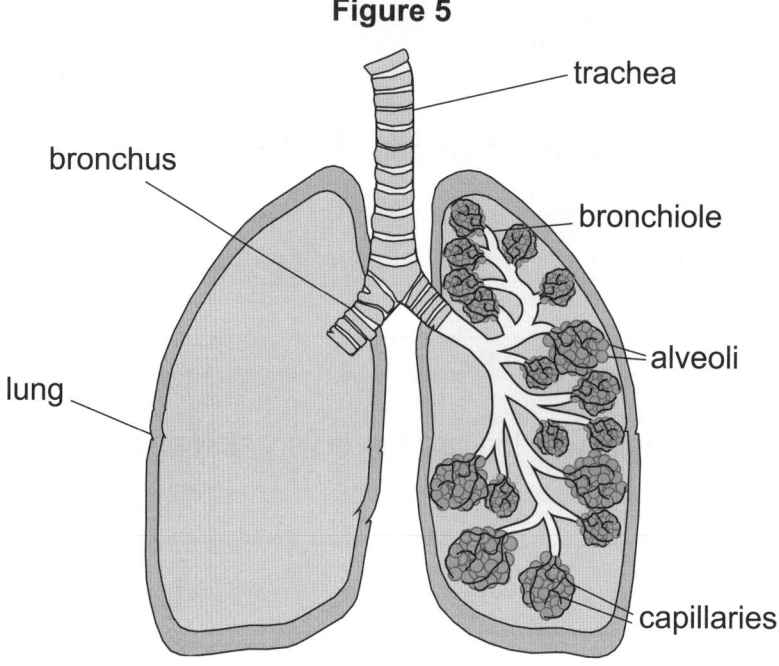

4.1   Capillaries are important in gas exchange.
Explain **one** way in which capillaries are adapted for this function.

....

....
[2 marks]

4.2   Carbon dioxide is present in the air that enters and leaves the lungs.
Explain why the air leaving the lungs contains more carbon dioxide than
the air entering them.

....

....

....
[2 marks]

4.3 Smoking can damage the lining of the trachea.
Explain why this means that people who smoke may be more likely to get lung infections than non-smokers.

....

....

....

....

....
[4 marks]

4.4 Smoking can reduce the surface area of the alveoli in the lungs.
Explain why this means that people who smoke may need to breathe more quickly when exercising than non-smokers.

....

....

....

....

....

....

....

....
[4 marks]

Turn over for the next question

Turn over ▶

5 A student investigated how the concentration of amylase affects the rate of digestion of starch into reducing sugars. He used Visking tubing in his experiment — this is a material which is permeable to small molecules, including reducing sugars.
This is the method he used:

1. He took three lengths of Visking tubing and tied one end of each into a knot.

2. He used a pipette to add starch solution to each length of tubing.

3. Next, he used the same pipette to add different concentrations of amylase to the tubing.

4. Then he tied the remaining end of each length of tubing.

5. He filled a test tube with distilled water and placed one of the lengths of tubing into the test tube. He repeated this step for the other two lengths of tubing (as shown in **Figure 6**) and then started a stop clock.

Figure 6

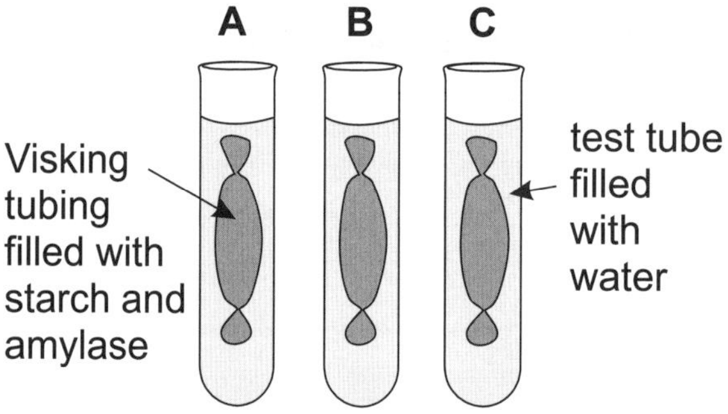

6. After 20 minutes he tested the water outside each length of tubing with Benedict's reagent.

His results are shown in **Table 2**.

Table 2

Tube	Colour of solution after Benedict's test
A	brick-red
B	green
C	yellow

5.1 Which tube showed the quickest rate of digestion? Explain your answer.

....

....

....

....

[3 marks]

5.2 Explain how the reducing sugars moved between the solution inside the Visking tubing and the surrounding water.

....

....

....

....

[2 marks]

5.3 Explain why it is important that each length of Visking tubing had the same surface area.

....

....

....

....

[2 marks]

5.4 Explain **one** problem with the student's method.

....

....

....

....

[2 marks]

Question 5 continues on the next page

Turn over ▶

Amylase is an important enzyme in the human body.

5.5 Give **two** places where amylase is produced in the body.

1. ....

2. ....

[2 marks]

5.6 Explain why it is important that starch is broken down into sugars in the digestive system.

....

....

....

[3 marks]

12

6 HPV is a virus. There are many different strains of HPV, some of which can cause cervical cancer in women.
A vaccine given to young women can help to protect against two cancer-causing strains of the virus and therefore reduce the occurrence of cervical cancer.

6.1 Explain how the HPV vaccine may help to protect a woman against cervical cancer.

....

....

....

....

....

....

....

....

....

[4 marks]

6.2 Explain how vaccinations may help to prevent the spread of the HPV virus in a population.

....

....

....

....

[2 marks]

Question 6 continues on the next page

Turn over ▶

In September 2008, the National Health Service in the UK began a programme of vaccinating teenage girls against HPV.

Figure 7 shows the percentage of sexually active young women between the ages of 16 and 18 who had the virus in 2008 and in the years between 2010 and 2013.

Figure 7

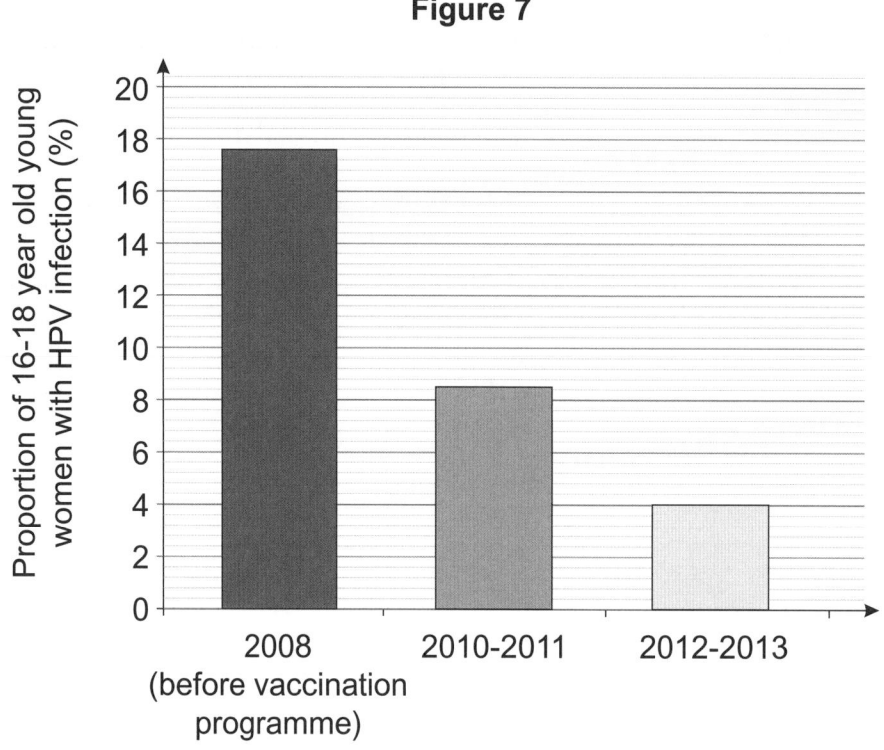

6.3   A scientist tested a random sample of **2000** sexually active 16-18 year old young women in 2008 for HPV.
Calculate how many of these young women would be expected to have a HPV infection.

Number expected to have HPV infection = ...
[2 marks]

The NHS spent £18.9 million in implementing the HPV vaccination in 2008/09.

The vaccine commonly causes minor side effects, including soreness at the site of injection. In very rare cases there may be more serious side effects, including difficulty breathing.

6.4 Evaluate the use of the vaccination programme against HPV in the UK, between 2008 and 2013. Use the information above and in **Figure 7**. Your answer should include a justified conclusion.

....

....

....

....

....

....

....

....

[4 marks]

6.5 Suggest **two** risk factors other than viruses which may increase a person's chance of getting cancer.

1. ....

2. ....

[2 marks]

Turn over for the next question

7   A scientist carries out an experiment to investigate which disinfectant, from a choice of five, is most effective against bacteria found on the work surface of a laboratory.

Before she begins her investigation, she wipes a swab across the work surface and then gently wipes the swab on the surface of an agar plate.
She incubates the agar plate for three days.

After incubation, a colony of bacteria has grown on the agar plate.
The scientist measures the diameter of the colony as 12.0 mm.

7.1   Calculate the area of the bacterial colony on the agar plate.
Give your answer to 3 significant figures.
Use the equation:

Area = πr^2

Area = ...mm^2
[2 marks]

The mean division time of one bacterial cell in the sample is 24 minutes.

7.2   Calculate how many cells there will be if one bacterial cell is left to divide for 4 hours.

.... cells
[2 marks]

The scientist cultures the bacteria she collected from the work surface in a liquid broth. She uses this to test the effectiveness of the disinfectants. This is an outline of the method she uses:

1. She passes an inoculating loop through the flame of a Bunsen burner and then uses it to spread the bacteria from the broth over a sterile agar plate.

2. She soaks five paper discs in five different disinfectants and places them on the agar plate.

3. She also places one paper disc that has not been soaked in disinfectant onto the agar plate.

4. She covers the agar plate with a lid and places it upside down in an incubator at 25 °C.

5. After a period of time she removes the agar plate from the incubator.

7.3 Explain why the scientist passed the inoculating loop through the flame of a Bunsen burner.

....

....

....

[2 marks]

7.4 Give **two** safety precautions that the scientist should have taken when working with the Bunsen burner.

1. ....

2. ....

[2 marks]

7.5 Explain how the scientist will determine which disinfectant is the most effective.

....

....

....

[2 marks]

Turn over for the next question

Turn over ▶

8   A farmer has decided to grow some of his plants in a greenhouse. Keeping the plants in the greenhouse means that they are kept at a higher temperature than they would be outside.

Figure 8 shows how the rate of photosynthesis of the plants is affected by temperature.

Figure 8

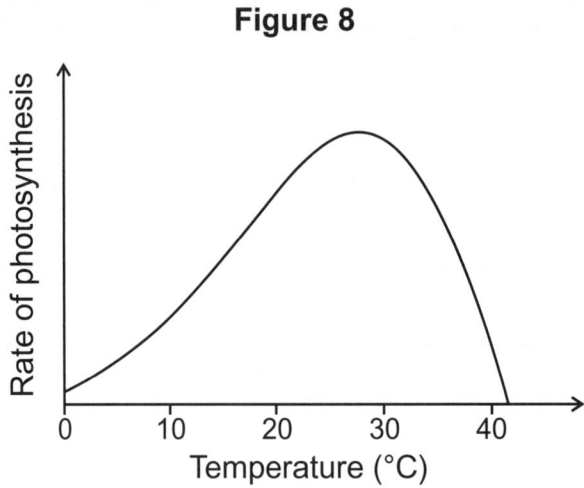

8.1   Explain the shape of the graph in **Figure 8**.

....

....

....

....

....

....

....

[4 marks]

The farmer places some lamps in his greenhouse approximately 1 m above his plants.

Figure 9 shows the effect of light intensity on the rate of photosynthesis when the plants are kept at 30 °C.

Figure 9

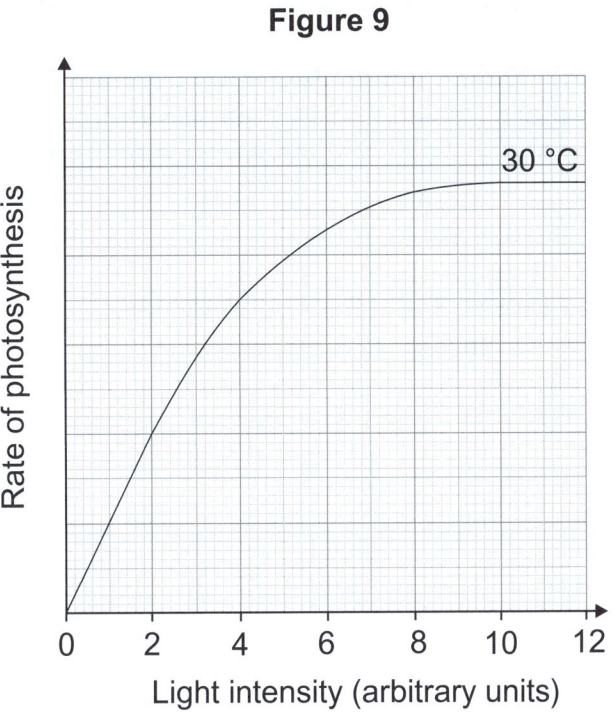

8.2 Draw the shape of the curve that you would expect to see if the plants were grown at 15 °C on **Figure 9**.

[2 marks]

Figure 10 shows the inverse square law for light intensity.
This law links light intensity and distance from a light source.

Figure 10

$$\text{light intensity} \propto \frac{1}{\text{distance } (d)^2}$$

The farmer moves the lamps in his greenhouse from 1 m to 0.5 m above his plants.

8.3 Which of the following statements about the change in light intensity reaching the plants is **true**?
Tick **one** box.

☐ The light intensity will be two times smaller than it was before.

☐ The light intensity will be four times smaller than it was before.

☐ The light intensity will be two times greater than it was before.

☐ The light intensity will be four times greater than it was before.

[1 mark]

Question 8 continues on the next page

Turn over ▶

The farmer wants to control conditions inside his greenhouse in order to make a greater profit from his plants.

He decides to use the lamps in his greenhouse for 4 hours every evening for 3 months during the winter. He decides to keep the light intensity at a level of 11 arbitrary units during these periods. This costs £25 a month.

The farmer also sets the heaters to maintain a temperature of 30 °C for 3 months during the winter. This costs £140 per month.
The average outside temperature during the winter months is 4 °C.

8.4 Evaluate the farmer's decision to grow his plants under these conditions compared to growing the plants outside.
Use the information in **Figures 8** and **9** for your answer.
Remember to include a conclusion.

....

....

....

....

....

....

....

....

....

....

....

....

....

....
[6 marks]

END OF QUESTIONS

GCSE Biology

Set A Paper 2

Higher Tier

In addition to this paper you should have:	Centre name				
• A ruler.	Centre number				
• A calculator.	Candidate number				

Surname	
Other names	
Candidate signature	

Time allowed:
• 1 hour 45 minutes

Instructions to candidates
• Write your name and other details in the spaces provided above.
• Answer **all** questions in the spaces provided.
• Do all rough work on the paper.
• Cross out any work you do not want to be marked.

Information for candidates
• The marks available are given in brackets at the end of each question.
• There are 100 marks available for this paper.
• You are allowed to use a calculator.
• You should use good English and present your answers in a clear and organised way.

Advice to candidates
• In calculations show clearly how you worked out your answers.

For examiner's use						
Q	Attempt Nº			Q	Attempt Nº	
	1	2	3		1	2	3
1				6			
2				7			
3				8			
4				9			
5				10			
				Total			

Answer **all** questions in the spaces provided

1 Wing length in fruit flies is controlled by two alleles.

Vestigial (short) wings are caused by the allele '**n**'.
Normal length wings are caused by the allele '**N**'.

The vestigial wing allele is recessive to the normal wing allele.

1.1 What does it mean if an allele is recessive?
Tick **one** box.

- ☐ Two copies of the allele need to be present for the characteristic to be displayed.
- ☐ Only one copy of the allele needs to be present for the characteristic to be displayed.
- ☐ The allele only has a very small chance of being passed on to offspring.

[1 mark]

1.2 Two fruit flies with normal length wings are crossed.
Complete the Punnett square in **Figure 1** to show this cross.

Figure 1

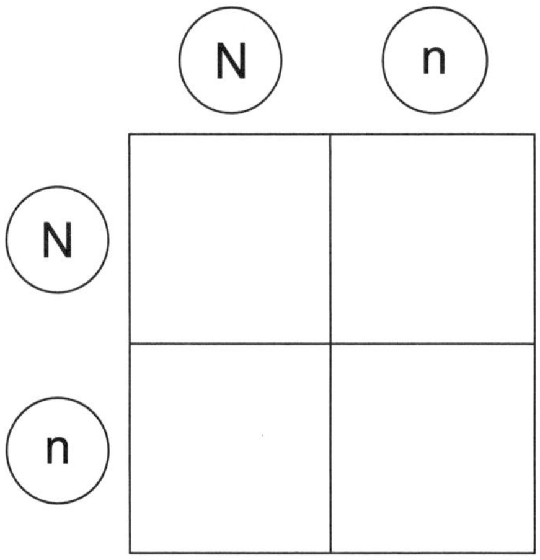

[2 marks]

1.3 The two fruit flies crossed in **Figure 1** have 200 offspring.
Calculate how many of the offspring would be expected to have vestigial wings.

Expected number of offspring with vestigial wings = ...
[2 marks]

1.4 Fruit flies are eukaryotic organisms.
Describe how the genetic material of a fruit fly is stored in its cells.

....

....

....

....

[3 marks]

Turn over for the next question

Turn over ▶

3

2 Quadrats can be used to investigate the distribution of organisms in a habitat. A group of students used 1 m² quadrats to investigate the plant species that live in a small field next to their school.

They divided the field up into three sections, as shown in **Figure 2**.

Figure 2

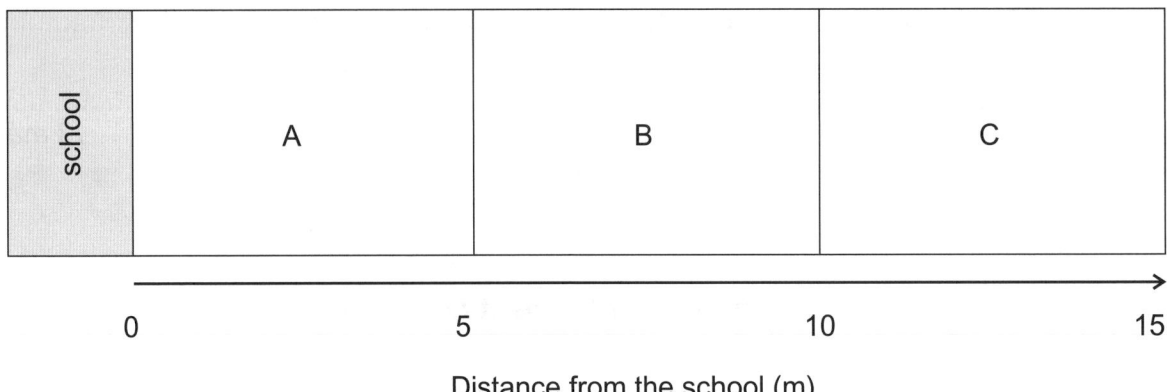

Distance from the school (m)

They placed three quadrats at random in each section of the field and counted the number of buttercups, clover and dandelions in each quadrat. Their results are shown in **Table 1**.

Table 1

Plant	Number counted per m²											
	Section A				Section B				Section C			
	1	2	3	Mean	1	2	3	Mean	1	2	3	Mean
Buttercups	54	50	52	52	60	65	64	63	80	94	90	88
Clover	70	74	69	71	87	96	88		121	129	131	127
Dandelions	3	5	4	4	5	7	9	7	13	12	11	12

2.1 Explain why the quadrats were placed randomly.

....

....
[1 mark]

2.2 What is the median number of buttercups per m² in section **A**?

median number of buttercups per m² in section **A** = ...
[1 mark]

2.3 Calculate the mean number of clover per m² in section **B**.
Give your answer to 2 significant figures.

Mean number of clover per m² = ...
[2 marks]

2.4 Section **C** measures 5 m by 3 m.
Use the data in **Table 1** to estimate the total population of dandelions in section **C**.

Estimated total population of dandelions in section **C** = ...
[2 marks]

2.5 Use the data in **Table 1** to give a conclusion about the distribution of the
three plant species across the field.

....

....
[1 mark]

2.6 Give **three** examples of abiotic factors that may affect the number of plants of each
species growing at different locations in the field.

1. ....

2. ....

3. ....
[3 marks]

Turn over for the next question

Turn over ▶

5

3   Students carried out an experiment to investigate the effect of age on reaction time. This is the method they used.

1.   They recruited 35 volunteers with ages between 20 and 60.

2.   The volunteers were asked to complete a task on a computer. In the task they had to press the enter key every time a certain shape appeared on the screen.

3.   Each volunteer completed the task 10 times and the mean reaction rate for each volunteer was calculated.

4.   The students then divided the volunteers' results into four age groups and calculated a mean reaction time for each group.

The results of the experiment are shown in **Table 2**.

Table 2

Age group	Number of volunteers	Mean reaction time (s)
20-29	12	0.30
30-39	5	0.31
40-49	12	0.35
50-60	6	0.39

The students' experiment tested a nervous response in the volunteers.

3.1   The effector in the response is a muscle in the hand.
Describe how muscles respond when they are stimulated by a nervous impulse.

....

[1 mark]

3.2   A motor neurone is involved in this nervous response.
Describe the role of motor neurones in the human body.

....

....

[2 marks]

3.3 Calculate the percentage increase in mean reaction time between the 20-29 age group and the 50-60 age group.

percentage increase = ...%

[2 marks]

3.4 Use data from **Table 2** to draw a bar chart on **Figure 3**, showing the mean reaction time for each age group.

- Complete the *y*-axis. Include a label and use a suitable scale.
- Plot the mean reaction time data.

Figure 3

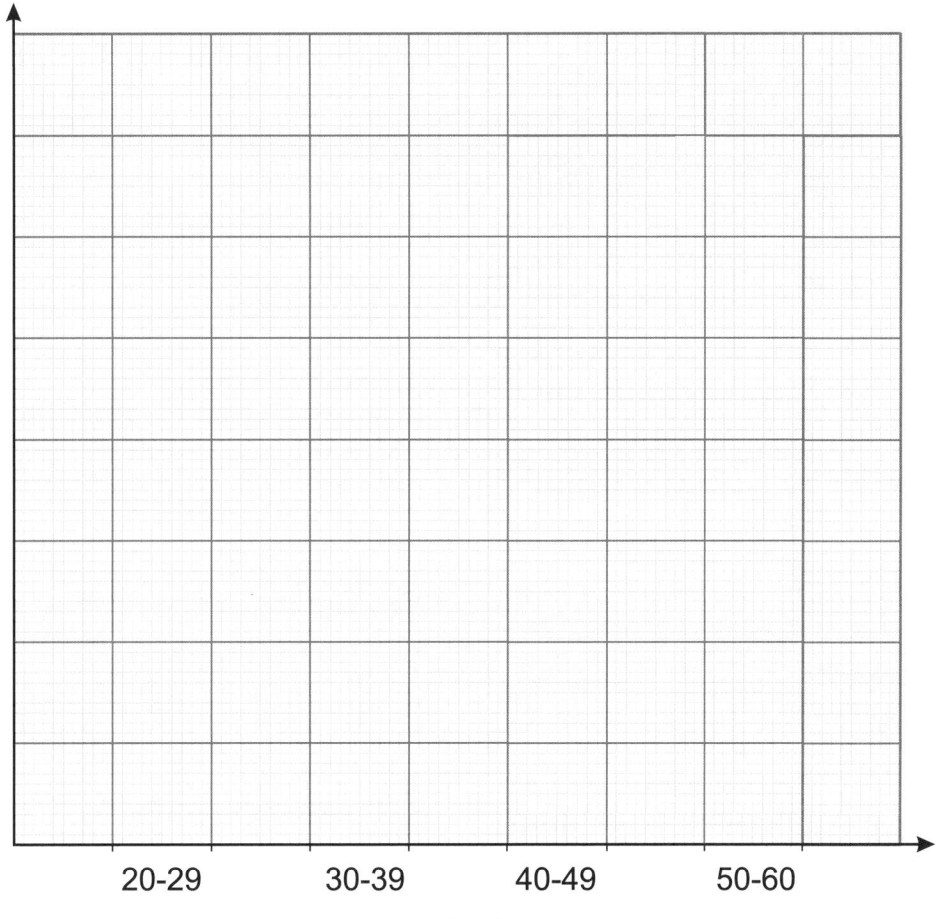

Age of volunteers

[2 marks]

Question 3 continues on the next page

Turn over ▶

From their results, the students concluded that as age increases, reaction time slows down.

3.5   Suggest **two** ways in which the students could have improved their method in order to have more confidence in their conclusion.

1. ....

....

2. ....

....

[2 marks]

4 A hospital patient has a suspected brain injury. Doctors have been running tests to determine which area of the patient's brain may have been damaged.

4.1 The patient is breathing normally without any medical assistance.
Using this information, suggest what part of the brain remains undamaged.
Explain your answer.

....

....

[2 marks]

Tests have shown that the patient's cerebral cortex has been damaged.
Figure 4 shows a diagram of the brain.

Figure 4

4.2 Which label on **Figure 4** corresponds to the cerebral cortex?
Tick **one** box.

☐ **A**

☐ **B**

☐ **C**

[1 mark]

4.3 Give **two** activities that are associated with the cerebral cortex.

1. ....

2. ....

[2 marks]

Question 4 continues on the next page

Turn over ▶

Another patient in the hospital has OPCA.
OPCA is a condition that affects the function of particular areas of the brain.
Symptoms include clumsiness, difficulty walking and loss of balance.

4.4 Using the information given above, suggest a region of the brain that may not be functioning normally in people suffering from OPCA. Explain your answer.

....

....

[2 marks]

4.5 Give **two** methods scientists can use to work out the function of particular parts of the brain.

1. ....

2. ....

[2 marks]

5   Plant hormones control aspects of a plant's growth.
       Some plant hormones are affected by factors outside of the plant, such as light.

       A student carried out an experiment to investigate how shoot growth is affected
       by light. A diagram of the experiment is shown in **Figure 5**.

Figure 5

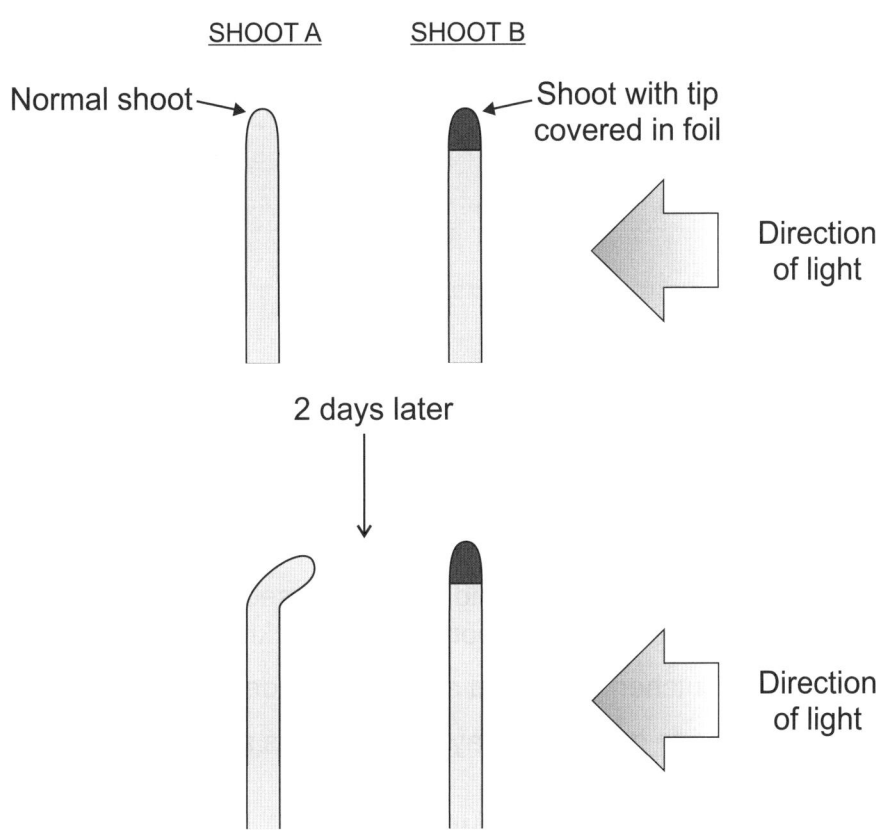

5.1   Name the response shown by shoot **A** after 2 days.

....

[1 mark]

5.2   Give **one** variable that the student should have controlled during the experiment.

....

[1 mark]

Question 5 continues on the next page

Turn over ▶

11

5.3 Explain the results of the student's experiment.

Leave blank

....

....

....

....

....

....

....

....

[4 marks]

The student carried out another experiment to investigate plant growth.

1. He placed a seedling on some damp kitchen towel.
2. He folded the kitchen towel over and gently pressed it so the seedling was secured inside. He secured the open ends of the kitchen towel with paper clips.
3. He then hung the kitchen towel and seedling upside down in a dark cupboard.
4. He left the seedling to grow for 5 days. His results are shown in **Figure 6**.

Figure 6

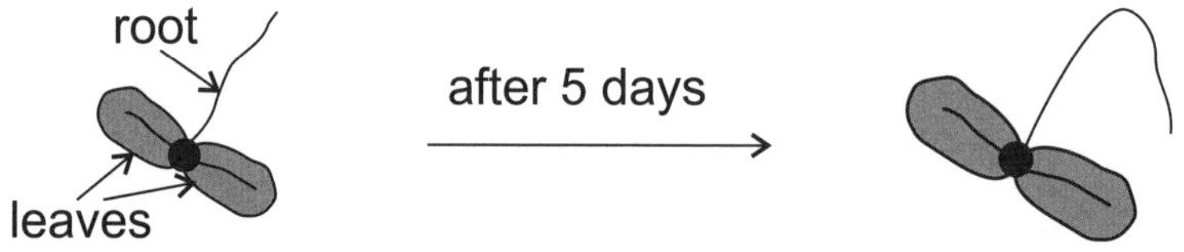

5.4 Explain the pattern of growth shown by the seedling's root.

....

....

....

....

....

[4 marks]

Auxin, gibberellin and ethene are all plant hormones that are used in agriculture and horticulture to control plant growth.

5.5 Describe how auxin can be used to help plants grow from cuttings.

....

....

[1 mark]

5.6 Give **three** ways that gibberellin can be used to control plant growth.

1. ....

2. ....

3. ....

[3 marks]

5.7 Explain **one** way in which ethene is used in the food industry.

....

....

....

[2 marks]

Turn over for the next question

Turn over ▶

13

6 A crop plant has been genetically modified to make it resistant to a particular herbicide. The GM crop plant contains a gene for herbicide resistance taken from another plant species.

6.1 The gene for herbicide resistance codes for a protein.
Explain how a gene can code for a protein.

....

....

[2 marks]

6.2 Explain how genetic engineering would have been used to produce the GM crop plant.

....

....

....

....

[3 marks]

The GM crop plant is already being grown by some farmers.

There are concerns that, as a result, wild grasses growing near to the crop plant might have also become more resistant to herbicides. Some scientists carried out an investigation to discover whether this had happened.

The scientists sprayed herbicide onto 100 grass plants in an area next to the GM crop, and onto 100 grass plants from a second area 2 km away from the GM crop.

Their results are shown in **Table 3**.

Table 3

Number of grass plants dying after spraying	
In area next to GM crop	**In area 2 km away from GM crop**
83	85

6.3 Explain the reason for testing a group of plants that had not been growing near the GM crop.

....

....

[2 marks]

14

6.4　Suggest **one** way in which the scientists could check if their results are reproducible.

....

....

[1 mark]

6.5　The scientists decided that there was no significant difference between the two groups of plants. Explain whether you agree or disagree with this conclusion.

....

....

[1 mark]

6.6　If the scientists are right in their conclusion, does this prove that the concerns about genes for resistance spreading are unfounded? Explain your answer.

....

....

....

....

[2 marks]

Turn over for the next question

Turn over ▶

7   **Figure 7** shows a marine food web found near a hydrothermal vent.

Figure 7

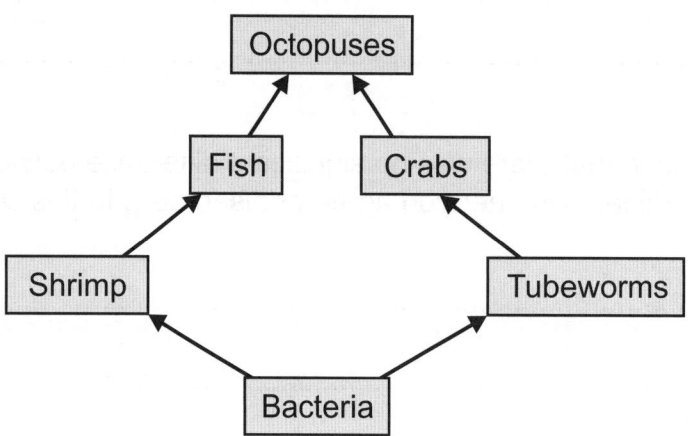

The producers in **Figure 7** are bacteria. They get the energy they need to increase their biomass from chemicals produced in the hydrothermal vent.

7.1   Compare these bacterial producers with typical plant producers.

....

....

....
[2 marks]

The bacteria in **Figure 7** can survive at temperatures over 100 °C.

7.2   What name is given to microorganisms that can survive in extreme conditions?

....
[1 mark]

7.3   Suggest **one** way in which the bacteria in **Figure 7** will be adapted to survive in such high temperatures. Explain your answer.

....

....

....
[2 marks]

The organisms in the food web in **Figure 7** are all interdependent.

7.4 Explain how a fall in the population of **tubeworms** could affect the population sizes of the other organisms in **Figure 7**.

....

....

....

....

....

....

....

....

....

[4 marks]

Turn over for the next question

Turn over ▶

8 **Figure 8** shows the blood water content of a person over a period of several hours.

Figure 8

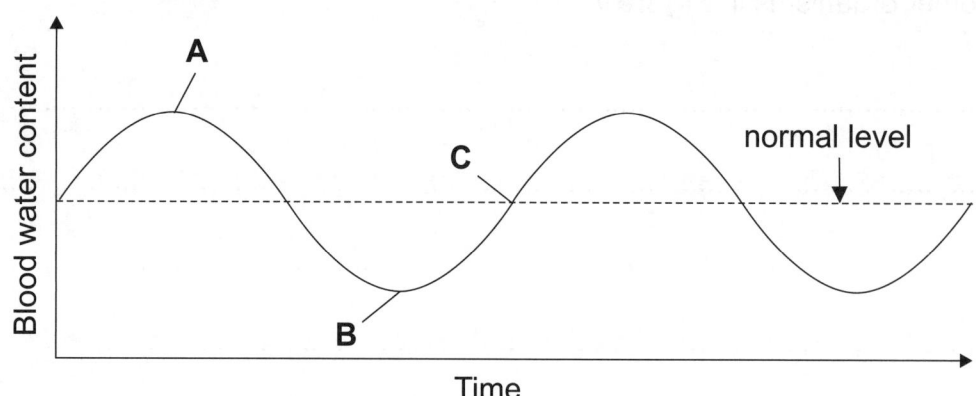

8.1 At which of the points on **Figure 8**, **A**, **B** or **C**, is the hormone ADH most likely to be released? Explain your answer.

Point at which ADH is most likely to be released ....

Explanation ....

....

....

....

[3 marks]

8.2 Name the gland that ADH is released from.

....

[1 mark]

8.3 Describe the effect that the release of ADH will have on the concentration of the person's urine.

....

[1 mark]

18

8.4 Suggest **two** reasons why the blood water content may have fallen to the level seen at point **B** on **Figure 8**.

1. ....

2. ....

[2 marks]

8.5 Explain why it is important that the water content of the blood is controlled.

....

....

....

[2 marks]

Turn over for the next question

Turn over ▶

9 In 1996, scientists at the Roslin Institute in Edinburgh, cloned a sheep. The sheep, Dolly, was the first mammal ever to be successfully cloned using adult cell cloning.

9.1 Describe the process used to produce Dolly the sheep.

....

....

....

....

....

....

....

....

....

....

....

[5 marks]

20

Since Dolly the sheep, other mammals such as pigs and cows have been successfully cloned using adult cell cloning. Cloning animals with desirable traits, such as high meat yield, could be used in agriculture rather than traditional methods of breeding.

9.2 Evaluate the use of cloning animals in agriculture rather than using traditional methods of breeding. Include a justified conclusion.

....

....

....

....

....

....

....

....

....

....

[4 marks]

Turn over for the next question

Turn over ▶

21

10 Fossils help to show us how organisms on Earth have evolved. However, it is difficult for scientists to determine how life on Earth began as the fossil record is incomplete.

10.1 Give **two** reasons why the fossil record is incomplete.

1. ....

2. ....

[2 marks]

In 2005, scientists reported having found fossilised chimpanzee teeth. The teeth were the first known chimpanzee fossils to be found.

10.2 Suggest how the chimpanzee teeth became fossilised.

....

....

....

....

[2 marks]

22

The chimpanzee and bonobo are two separate species that evolved from a common ancestor.

It is thought that two populations of the ancestor became isolated from each other when the Congo River formed. The population to the north of the river became chimpanzees and the population to the south became bonobos.

10.3 Use your knowledge of natural selection and speciation to suggest how the new species of chimpanzee and bonobo evolved from the same common ancestor.

....

....

....

....

....

....

....

....

....

....

....

[6 marks]

END OF QUESTIONS

GCSE Biology

Set B Paper 2

Higher Tier

In addition to this paper you should have:
- A ruler.
- A calculator.

Centre name				
Centre number				
Candidate number				

Time allowed:
- 1 hour 45 minutes

Surname	
Other names	
Candidate signature	

Instructions to candidates
- Write your name and other details in the spaces provided above.
- Answer **all** questions in the spaces provided.
- Do all rough work on the paper.
- Cross out any work you do not want to be marked.

Information for candidates
- The marks available are given in brackets at the end of each question.
- There are 100 marks available for this paper.
- You are allowed to use a calculator.
- You should use good English and present your answers in a clear and organised way.

Advice to candidates
- In calculations show clearly how you worked out your answers.

For examiner's use

Q	Attempt Nº			Q	Attempt Nº		
	1	2	3		1	2	3
1				6			
2				7			
3				8			
4				9			
5				10			
				Total			

1

Answer **all** questions in the spaces provided

1   Most cells in the human body contain chromosomes.

1.1   How many pairs of chromosomes are there in a typical human body cell?

....

[1 mark]

All of a human's genome is found within chromosomes.

1.2   Define the term **genome**.

....

[1 mark]

Two chromosomes in each human body cell are sex chromosomes.

1.3   Describe how sex chromosomes differ between a male and a female.

....

....

[2 marks]

Sperm cells only have one copy of each chromosome.

1.4   Which process causes sperm cells to only have one copy of each chromosome?
          Tick **one** box.

          ☐ differentiation

          ☐ mitosis

          ☐ meiosis

          ☐ mutation

[1 mark]

1.5   During sexual reproduction, a sperm cell and an egg cell fuse together to form
          a new cell. Describe how this new cell develops into a new organism.

....

....

....

....

[3 marks]

2 Diabetes is a condition in which the body cannot effectively control its blood glucose level.

2.1 Which organ in the body is responsible for monitoring the blood glucose level?

....
[1 mark]

In 2015, it was estimated that **1 in 16** people in the UK had either Type 1 or Type 2 diabetes.

2.2 The English town of Derby had a population of approximately **260 000** people in 2015.
Calculate the approximate number of people in Derby who had either Type 1 or Type 2 diabetes at this time.

number of people = ...
[1 mark]

The number of people with **Type 2** diabetes in the UK has been rising for many years.

2.3 Suggest **one** reason why a rise in unhealthy diets may have led to an increase in the number of people with **Type 2** diabetes.

....

....
[1 mark]

2.4 Give **two** ways in which **Type 2** diabetes can be controlled.

1. ....

2. ....
[2 marks]

Question 2 continues on the next page

Turn over ▶

3

A man has **Type 1** diabetes. He treats his condition by regularly injecting himself with insulin.

2.5 Explain why it is necessary for the man to regularly inject insulin.

....

....

....

[2 marks]

The man was asked by his doctor to monitor his blood glucose level over the course of a day. **Figure 1** shows some of the data he collected.

Figure 1

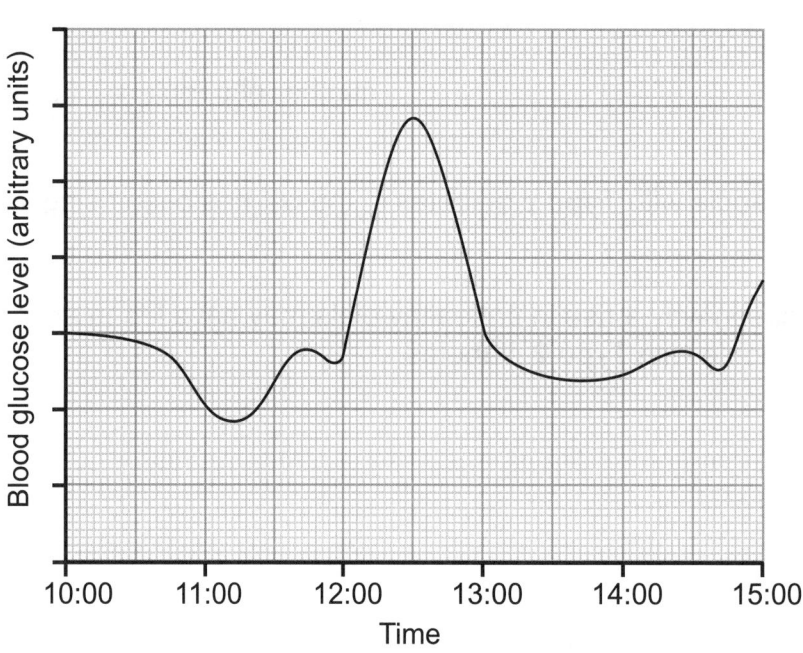

In the time period shown on **Figure 1** the man injected himself with insulin once.

2.6 What time is the man most likely to have injected insulin?
Tick **one** box.

☐ 10:00

☐ 12:00

☐ 12:30

☐ 13:00

[1 mark]

Leav
blan

3   **Figure 2** shows a Labradoodle.
Labradoodles are dogs that have been bred from a Labrador retriever and a poodle.

Figure 2

A Labrador retriever's gentle temperament makes them popular as guide dogs for people with sight difficulties.

However, Labrador retrievers shed a lot of hair, so they can be unsuitable for people with dog allergies.

Labradoodles were first created in order to provide guide dogs for people with dog allergies.

3.1   Suggest **one** characteristic of poodles which first encouraged breeders to cross one with a Labrador retriever.

....

[1 mark]

Question 3 continues on the next page

Turn over ▶

When a Labrador retriever is crossed with a poodle, the results are varied.

Some of the puppies do not have the right temperament for being a guide dog.
Some of the puppies are not suitable for people with dog allergies.

3.2 Describe how Labradoodle guide dogs, which are suitable for people with dog allergies, could be consistently produced using selective breeding.

....

....

....

....

....

....

....

[3 marks]

3.3 Describe **two** disadvantages of using selective breeding to create dog breeds such as Labradoodles.

1. ....

....

2. ....

....

[2 marks]

GCSE AQA Biology / Set B / Paper 2

6

© CGP 2017 — copying more than
5% of this paper is not permitted

4 Food security ensures there is enough food to feed the human population.

4.1 Describe **three** biological factors that threaten food security around the world.

1. ....

....

2. ....

....

3. ....

....

[3 marks]

Figure 3 shows three different food chains that help to feed the human population.

Figure 3

A   grass $\longrightarrow$ cattle $\longrightarrow$ human

B   pondweed $\longrightarrow$ small fish $\longrightarrow$ salmon $\longrightarrow$ human

C   wheat $\longrightarrow$ human

4.2 Which of the food chains in **Figure 3** (**A**, **B** or **C**) shows the most efficient food production for humans? Explain your answer.

Food chain ....

Explanation ....

....

[2 marks]

Look at food chain **A** in **Figure 3**.
The biomass of the grass is 8000 arbitrary units.
The biomass of the cattle is 700 arbitrary units.

4.3 Calculate the efficiency of biomass transfer between the grass and the cattle.
Use the equation:

$$\text{efficiency} = \frac{\text{biomass transferred to the next level}}{\text{biomass available at the previous level}} \times 100$$

efficiency = ... %
[1 mark]

Question 4 continues on the next page

Turn over ▶

Turkeys are farmed to provide meat for humans to eat.

Many turkey farmers increase the efficiency of meat production by controlling the conditions in which they keep their birds.

Table 1 lists some of the rearing conditions for 20 week old turkeys at three different turkey farms. All the turkey farms rear the same type of turkey.

Table 1

	Turkey Farm		
	A	B	C
Space per bird (m^2)	0.55	0.85	0.47
Temperature of turkey shed (°C)	17	20	22

4.4 Based on the information in Table 1, suggest which turkey farm (A, B or C) produces turkey meat most efficiently. Explain your answer.

....

....

....

....

....

....

[4 marks]

8

5 Gregor Mendel proposed the idea of separate 'hereditary units'.

In one experiment he investigated the inheritance of round or wrinkled seed coats in pea plants. The allele for round seed coats (R) is dominant over the allele for wrinkled seed coats (r).

Mendel first crossed pure-breeding round seed plants (RR) with pure-breeding wrinkled seed plants (rr).

All the offspring of this cross had round seeds and a heterozygous genotype.

5.1 Explain how the experiment shows that the allele for round seeds is dominant.

....

....

....

[2 marks]

Mendel then crossed the heterozygous offspring together.

5.2 Draw a genetic diagram to show the predicted results of this cross.
Identify the phenotype of each offspring.

Phenotype of each offspring: ....

[3 marks]

Question 5 continues on the next page

Turn over ▶

When Mendel crossed the offspring, 7324 plants were produced.
5474 of these had round seed coats and the other 1850 had wrinkled seed coats.

5.3 Calculate the ratio of round to wrinkled seed coats in Mendel's results.
Give the ratio in its simplest form.
Give your answer to 3 significant figures.

ratio of round to wrinkled seed coats = ... : 1

[1 mark]

5.4 Suggest **one** reason why Mendel's proposal was not recognised
by scientists until after his death.

....

....

[1 mark]

6 An experiment was carried out to discover the best growth medium for the tissue culture of a certain species of plant. Four different growth media, **1 - 4**, were used. Each growth medium contained a different amount of a plant growth hormone.

Scientists cut five blocks of stem tissue, each measuring 1 mm × 1 mm × 1 mm. They then weighed each block using a mass balance.
The blocks were placed on **growth medium 1**, as shown in **Figure 4**.

Figure 4

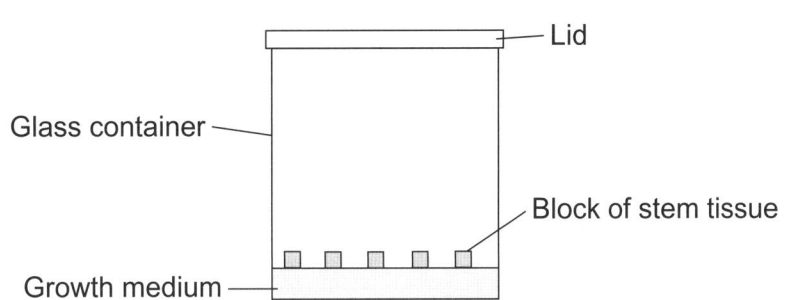

The container was then incubated at 35 °C for two days. At the end of that time, the blocks were taken out and weighed again to see how much they had grown.

This was repeated with the other three growth media.

The whole experiment was repeated twice again, using leaf tissue and then using root tissue instead of stem tissue.

The results for **growth medium 1** are shown in **Table 2**.

Table 2

Block number	percentage increase in mass (%)		
	Stem tissue	Leaf tissue	Root tissue
1	119	33	76
2	97	21	62
3	100	17	58
4	114	25	192
5	125	39	92
Mean	**X**	27	72

6.1 Circle the anomalous result in **Table 2**.

[1 mark]

6.2 Calculate the value of **X** in **Table 2**.

X = ...
[1 mark]

Question 6 continues on the next page

Turn over ▶

Use data from **Table 2** to draw a bar chart on **Figure 5**. The bar chart should show the mean percentage increase in mass for each tissue.

Leave blank

- Complete the axes. Include a label and a sensible scale for each.
- Plot the mean percentage increase in mass for each tissue type.

Figure 5

[2 marks]

6.4 The plant tissue samples showed the greatest increase in mass in **growth medium 4**.

In growth medium 4, all tissue samples increased by a ratio of **1 : 2.5** compared to the results for **growth medium 1**.

Calculate the percentage increase in mass for **root tissue** grown in growth medium 4. Use data from **Table 2**.

increase in mass = ...%
[1 mark]

12

6.5 Give the dependent variable in this experiment.

....

[1 mark]

6.6 Give **one** control variable in this experiment.

....

[1 mark]

6.7 Suggest **one** reason why it was important that the scientists put a lid on the glass container in which the blocks were incubated.

....

....

[1 mark]

6.8 The scientists could have measured the growth of the blocks using a ruler. Suggest why using a mass balance instead may have given them more valid results.

....

....

[1 mark]

6.9 Describe a control that could have been used in this experiment.

....

....

....

....

[2 marks]

Turn over for the next question

Turn over ▶

7 The Earth's temperature is gradually increasing as a result of global warming.

7.1 Describe **one** change to the Earth's atmosphere which is contributing to global warming.

....

[1 mark]

One effect of global warming is a change in bird migration patterns.

Swallows migrate across parts of Europe and arrive in Britain in spring.

Figure 6 shows two sets of data produced by different scientists studying the migration pattern of swallows.

Data set **1** was collected in a study that lasted 222 years.
Data set **2** was collected in a study that lasted 43 years.

In each study, the scientists recorded the first day in the year that a swallow was seen in Britain. These results have been plotted against the average April temperature in Britain that year.

Figure 6

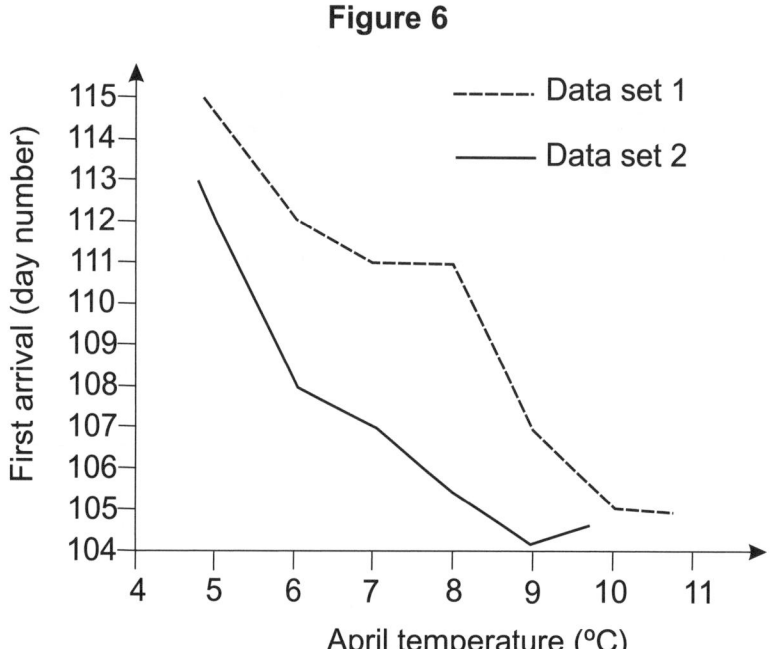

7.2 Describe the overall trend shown on **Figure 6**.

....

....

[1 mark]

7.3 Evaluate whether the results of the two studies, as shown by **Figure 6**, provide valid evidence that the migration pattern of swallows has been affected by global warming.

....

....

....

....

....

....

....

....

[4 marks]

Turn over for the next question

Turn over ▶

8   A woman's menstrual cycle is controlled by hormones.

8.1   Explain how hormones interact to control the menstrual cycle.

....

....

....

....

....

....

....

....

....

....

....

....

[6 marks]

8.2 Hormones are involved in *in vitro* fertilisation (IVF).
Describe the process of IVF.

....

....

....

....

....

....

....

[4 marks]

8.3 Describe **two** downsides of using fertility treatment such as IVF to try to have a baby.

1. ....

....

2. ....

....

[2 marks]

Turn over for the next question

Turn over ▶

9   **Figure 7** shows a diagram of the eye.

Figure 7

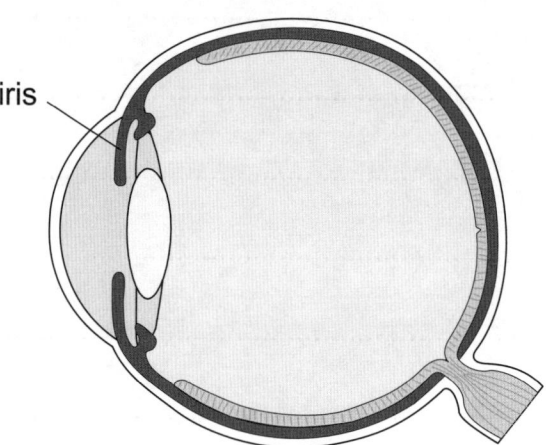

iris

9.1   Add labels to **Figure 7** to show a **suspensory ligament** and the **sclera**.

[2 marks]

9.2   Explain how the structure of the iris relates to its function.

....

....

....

[2 marks]

9.3   Explain how the eye adjusts to view **distant** objects.

....

....

....

....

....

[4 marks]

Figure 8 shows how rays of light enter the eye in a person with hyperopia.

Figure 8

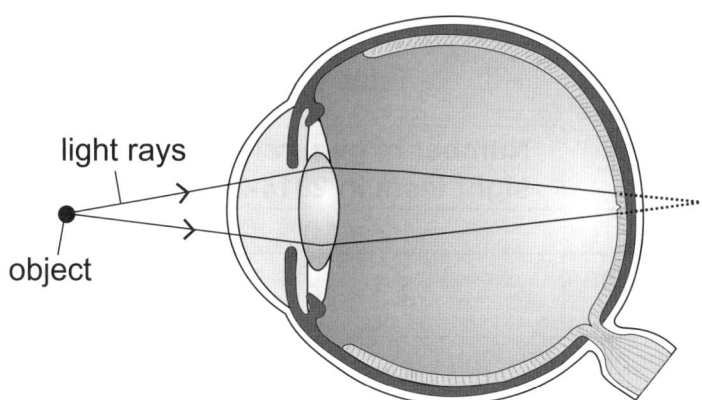

9.4   Complete **Figure 9** to show how the vision of a person with hyperopia can be corrected using glasses.
You should draw a lens and light rays on the diagram.

Figure 9

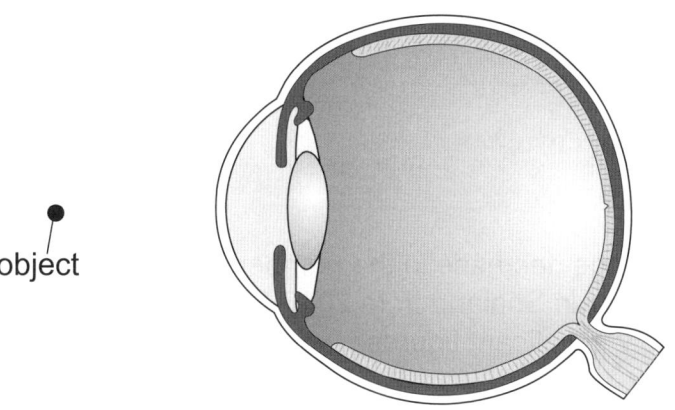

[2 marks]

Question 9 continues on the next page

Turn over ▶

19

Hyperopia can be diagnosed with a sight test.

Table 3 shows data about the number of general NHS sight tests carried out in England and Wales in 2014-2015.

Table 3

		Number of general NHS sight tests in 2014-2015	Change since 2013-2014
England	**Total**	1.3×10^7	-0.2%
	For children aged 0-15	2.7×10^6	$+7.5\%$
	For people aged 60+	5.5×10^6	-0.1 million
Wales	**Total**	7.5×10^5	-1.1%

9.5 Give **two** conclusions you can draw from the data in **Table 3**.

1. ....

....

2. ....

....

[2 marks]

9.6 Calculate the percentage decrease in the number of general NHS sight tests for people **aged 60 or over** in England from 2013-2014 to 2014-2015.
Give your answer to 2 significant figures.

percentage decrease = ...%
[3 marks]

20

10 An investigation was carried out into the abundance and distribution of earthworms around a dried up reservoir. **Figure 10** shows the study area as seen from above.

Figure 10

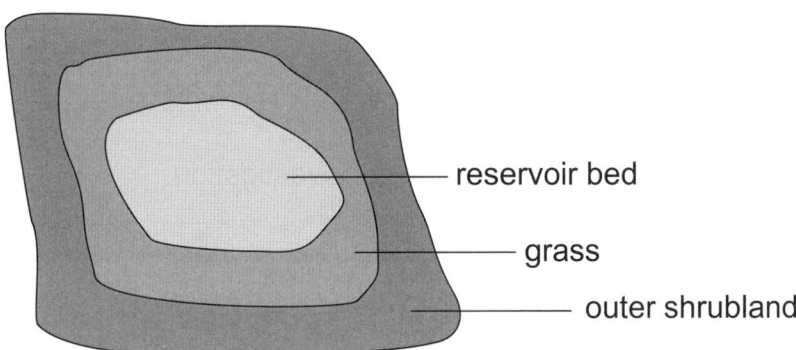

The scientists began by investigating the abundance of earthworms in the reservoir bed.

1. They placed ten quadrats, each with an area of 0.5 m², randomly in the area.

2. At each quadrat, they dug down to a depth of 0.3 m and collected the soil they removed.

3. They then searched through each soil sample and recorded the number of earthworms they found at each quadrat.

10.1 Describe what the scientists should have done next in order to calculate the abundance of earthworms in the reservoir bed.

....

....

....

[2 marks]

10.2 Suggest **one** way that the scientists could have got a more accurate estimate of the abundance of earthworms.

....

....

[1 mark]

Question 10 continues on the next page

Turn over ▶

10.3 Suggest **one** way the scientists could have ensured they were working ethically in this investigation.

....

....

[1 mark]

10.4 Suggest **one** source of error in the scientists' investigation.

....

....

[1 mark]

For the next part of their investigation, the scientists investigated the distribution of earthworms from the centre of the reservoir bed to the outer scrubland.

10.5 Describe a method the scientists could have used to produce valid results.

....

....

....

....

....

....

....

....

....

[4 marks]

The scientists also collected data about the organic material contained in the soil from the centre of the reservoir bed to the outer scrubland.

A summary of their results is shown in **Figure 11**.

Figure 11

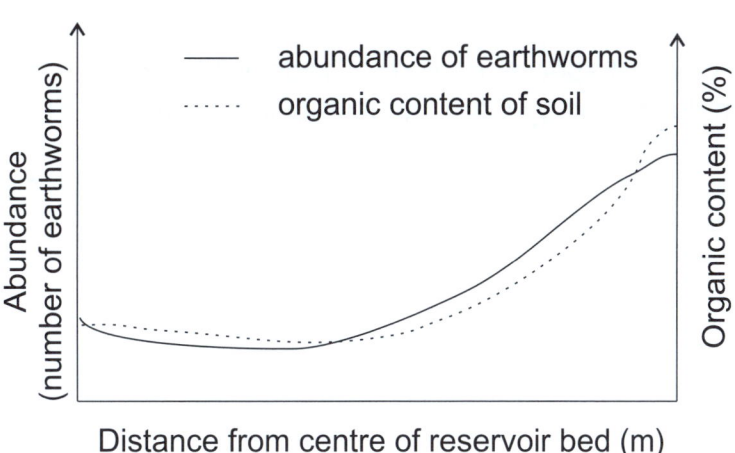

10.6 A scientist made the following conclusion based on the results of the investigation: "Soil containing high levels of organic material leads to a greater abundance of earthworms."
Give **one** reason why this is **not** a valid conclusion.

....

....
[1 mark]

Much of the organic matter found in soil is the remains of dead organisms. Earthworms feed on this organic material.

10.7 Explain how the earthworms feeding on organic material in the soil contributes to the carbon cycle.

....

....
[2 marks]

Question 10 continues on the next page

Turn over ▶

The scientists mainly found common earthworms in their investigation.
The Latin name for this species is *Lumbricus terrestris*.

10.8 What does the term *Lumbricus* refer to?

....

[1 mark]

There are many different species of worm. Traditionally worms were classified using the system developed by Carl Linnaeus in the 1700s.

10.9 Describe how developments in biology have enabled scientists to classify some organisms differently now than they did in the 1700s.

....

....

....

....

....

....

....

....

[4 marks]

END OF QUESTIONS

CGP

GCSE AQA

Biology

For the Grade 9-1 Course

Practice Exam Papers
Instructions & Answer Book

Higher Tier

Power up your exam performance with CGP!

Let's face it, AQA's Grade 9-1 GCSE Biology exams are tough. If you want to do well, you'll need to practise until you're a finely-honed exam-smashing superbeing.

Luckily, this brilliant pack from CGP includes two full sets of Practice Papers to help you beef up your exam muscles. We've made sure they're as realistic as possible, so you'll be ready for anything the examiners might have in store on the day.

Better still, this booklet contains full answers and mark schemes for all the papers, so it's easy to check how you're getting on. The exams will be sorry they messed with you.

What to Expect in The Exams

① Topics are Covered in Different Papers

For AQA GCSE Biology, you'll sit two exam papers at the end of your course.

Paper	Time	No. of marks	Specification Topics Assessed
1	1 hr 45 mins	100	1, 2, 3 and 4
2	1 hr 45 mins	100	5, 6 and 7

You're expected to know the basic concepts of biology in both papers.

② You'll be Tested on your Maths...

At least 10% of the total marks for AQA GCSE Biology come from questions on the maths skills you've used in the course. You'll be expected to calculate the mean and range for a set of data, so make sure you know how to do it for your exam.

③ ...and on your Practical Skills

- AQA GCSE Biology contains ten required practical activities that you'll do during the course — but you can also be asked about them in the exams.

- At least 15% of the total marks will be from questions testing practical skills.

- For example, you might be asked to comment on the design of an experiment (the apparatus and methods), make predictions, analyse or interpret results... Pretty much anything to do with planning and carrying out the investigations.

You could be asked about other practical activities as well. So you'll need to be able to apply the skills you've learnt for the required practicals to other experiments.

Marking Your Papers

- Do a complete exam set (Paper 1 and Paper 2).

- Use the answers and mark scheme in this booklet to mark each exam paper.

- Write down your mark for each paper in the table below
  — each paper is worth 100 marks.

- Find your total for the whole exam (out of a maximum of 200 marks)
  by adding up your marks from both papers.

- Follow the instructions below to estimate your grade.

	Paper 1	Paper 2	Total mark	Grade
SET A				
SET B				

Estimating Your Grade

- If you want to get a **rough idea** of the grade you're working at, we suggest you compare the **total mark** you got in **each set** to the latest set of grade boundaries.

- Grade boundaries are set for each individual exam, so they're likely to **change** from year to year. You can find the latest set of grade boundaries by going to
  www.cgpbooks.co.uk/gcsegradeboundaries

- Jot down the marks required for each grade in the table below so you don't have to refer back to the website. Use these marks to **estimate your grade**.
  If you're borderline, don't push yourself up a grade — the real examiners won't.

Total mark required for each grade						
Grade	9	8	7	6	5	4
Total mark out of 200						

- Remember, this will only be a **rough guide**, and grade boundaries will be different for different exams, but it should help you to see how you're getting on.

Published by CGP

Editors: Ciara McGlade, Rachael Rogers, Hayley Thompson.
Proofreader: Philip Armstrong.

Many thanks to Laura Jakubowski for the copyright research.

Clipart from Corel®
Illustrations by: Sandy Gardner Artist, email
sandy@sandygardner.co.uk
Printed by Elanders Ltd, Newcastle upon Tyne.
Text, design, layout and original illustrations
© Coordination Group Publications Ltd. (CGP) 2017
All rights reserved.

Answers

Set A — Paper 1

1.1 Gonorrhoea *[1 mark]*

1.2 Any two from: e.g. fever *[1 mark]* / stomach cramps *[1 mark]* / vomiting *[1 mark]* / diarrhoea *[1 mark]*.

1.3 Bacteria cause symptoms by producing toxins that damage the host's cells and tissues *[1 mark]*, whereas viruses cause symptoms by damaging host cells when they reproduce inside them *[1 mark]*.

1.4 Any two from: e.g. plasmids *[1 mark]* / single loop of DNA *[1 mark]* / no nucleus *[1 mark]*.

1.5 E.g. 4 μm = 0.004 mm
magnification = 18 ÷ 0.004 = × **4500**
OR
18 mm = 18 000 μm
magnification = 18 000 ÷ 4 = × **4500**
[2 marks for the correct answer, otherwise 1 mark for a correct conversion]

1.6 How to grade your answer:
Level 0: There is no relevant information. *[No marks]*
Level 1: There is a brief explanation of one or two ways in which the body defends itself against *Salmonella* infection after the pathogen has been ingested. *[1 to 2 marks]*
Level 2: There is a full explanation of several ways in which the body defends itself against *Salmonella* infection after the pathogen has been ingested. *[3 to 4 marks]*
Here are some points your answer may include:
The stomach produces hydrochloric acid.
The acid helps to kill most of the *Salmonella* bacteria that reach the stomach from the mouth.
White blood cells/the immune system will try to fight off *Salmonella* bacteria that reach the cells of the intestines.
For example, some white blood cells will carry out phagocytosis — this involves engulfing the bacteria and digesting them.
Other types of white blood cell will produce antibodies. These will lock on to the antigens on the *Salmonella* bacteria and cause them to be targeted for destruction by other white blood cells.
Other types of white blood cell will produce antitoxins. These will neutralise the toxins produced by the *Salmonella*.

2.1 oxygen *[1 mark]*
Remember, plants give off oxygen when they photosynthesise.

2.2 The volume of gas collected would decrease *[1 mark]* because when the lamp is turned off the light intensity will decrease *[1 mark]*, so the rate of photosynthesis will decrease too *[1 mark]*.

2.3 Carbon dioxide is needed for photosynthesis *[1 mark]*, so adding it to the water ensures that the rate of photosynthesis is not limited by a lack of carbon dioxide *[1 mark]*.

2.4 1 hour = 60 minutes
rate of photosynthesis = volume ÷ time
= 8.0 ÷ 60
= 0.1333... = **0.13 cm³/min** (2 s.f.)
[2 marks for the correct answer, otherwise 1 mark for the correct working or 1 mark for 0.1333...]

2.5 E.g. it may have affected/increased the activity of the enzymes in the pondweed that control photosynthesis *[1 mark]*.
Increasing the temperature will also have increased the energy of the reacting particles and speed at which they move about (making successful collisions between them more likely). If you'd remembered this bit of particle theory from chemistry and used it in your answer, you'd have also got the mark.

2.6 E.g. by putting the beaker into a warm water bath to keep the temperature constant *[1 mark]*.

2.7 E.g. using a measuring cylinder should give more accurate results *[1 mark]*.

2.8 Any three from: e.g. for respiration / for making cellulose for cell walls / for making amino acids/proteins / to store as starch / to convert into fats and oils for storage.
[3 marks — 1 mark for each correct answer]

3.1 Starch is broken down by the enzyme amylase *[1 mark]* into simple sugars *[1 mark]*.

3.2 E.g. add iodine solution to the sample *[1 mark]*. If the iodine solution remains browny-orange then the starch has been broken down. / If the iodine solution turns black/blue-black then the starch has not been broken down *[1 mark]*.

3.3 Liver *[1 mark]*

3.4 Bile emulsifies fat/breaks fat down into tiny droplets *[1 mark]*. This gives a larger surface area for enzymes/lipases to work on and so the fat is digested more quickly *[1 mark]*. By blocking the bile ducts, the gallstones could prevent bile from entering the small intestine *[1 mark]*. If so, any fat may be digested more slowly, possibly causing problems *[1 mark]*.

4.1 Oxygen moves into cells by diffusion *[1 mark]*. There's a net movement of oxygen from a higher concentration outside the cell to a lower concentration of oxygen inside the cell *[1 mark]* through the partially permeable cell membrane *[1 mark]*.

4.2 The rate of oxygen movement across the cell membrane will increase *[1 mark]*. This is because the cell will be using more oxygen (due to the increased rate of aerobic respiration) *[1 mark]*. This will make the concentration gradient of oxygen across the cell membrane steeper/increase the difference in the concentration of oxygen between the inside and outside of the cell *[1 mark]*.

4.3 As single-celled organisms, *Euglena* have a relatively large surface area to volume ratio *[1 mark]*. This means they can absorb enough oxygen to survive by diffusion through their outer surface alone *[1 mark]*. However, as multicellular organisms, trout have a relatively small surface area to volume ratio *[1 mark]*. Diffusion of oxygen across their outer surface would be too slow to supply all their needs, so trout need specialised exchange organs in order to absorb enough oxygen to survive *[1 mark]*.

5.1 As the rate of work increases the cyclist's blood lactic acid concentration also increases *[1 mark]*. At higher rates of work the cyclist's blood lactic acid concentration increases more quickly *[1 mark]*.

5.2 During vigorous exercise the body can't supply enough oxygen to the muscles, so they start to respire anaerobically as well as aerobically *[1 mark]*. Anaerobic respiration produces lactic acid *[1 mark]*. The harder the muscles work, the more they'll resort to anaerobic respiration and the more lactic acid they'll produce *[1 mark]*.

5.3 The cyclist's pulse rate and breathing rate will remain high after her race *[1 mark]*. This is because after vigorous exercise the body has an oxygen debt *[1 mark]*. Her pulse rate and breathing rate remain high to supply enough oxygen to react with the build up of lactic acid and so remove it from the cells *[1 mark]*.

5.4 A group of cells in the right atrium of the heart act as a pacemaker *[1 mark]*.

6.1 Malignant tumours invade neighbouring tissues / spread to different parts of the body forming secondary tumours *[1 mark]*, whereas benign tumours are contained within one area and do not spread to other parts of the body *[1 mark]*.

6.2

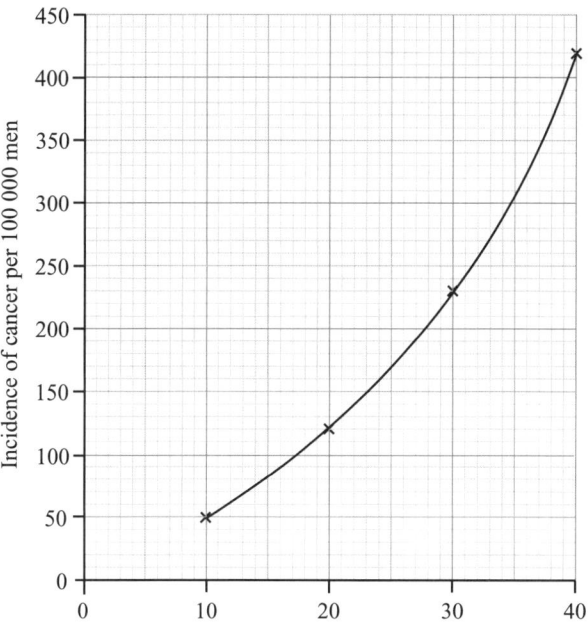

Number of cigarettes smoked per day

[3 marks — 1 mark for choosing a label and suitable scale for the y-axis, 1 mark for plotting all data points correctly, 1 mark for drawing a smooth curve of best fit.]

When you're drawing a curve or line of best fit on a graph, you shouldn't extend it past the plotted points. That's why the curve on this graph hasn't been extended to the origin (the point where the axes meet).

6.3 No. E.g. the data shows the incidence of cancer, not deaths from cancer *[1 mark]*. The data also only shows the incidence of cancer in men not women, so you can't say this trend is true for everyone *[1 mark]*. Finally the data is only given for smokers, so you can't compare the likelihood of developing cancer in smokers and non-smokers *[1 mark]*.

7.1 % change = (final height – original height) ÷ original height
$$\times\,100$$
$$= (7-4) \div 4 \times 100 = \textbf{75\%}$$
[2 marks for correct answer, otherwise 1 mark for correct working]

7.2 Beaker B was low in nitrates *[1 mark]*. Nitrates are needed for making amino acids/proteins *[1 mark]*, which are essential for growth *[1 mark]*.

7.3 It would have yellow leaves *[1 mark]* because without magnesium the plant can't make the chlorophyll that gives it its green colour *[1 mark]*.

7.4 Any two from: e.g. the amount of light shining on each beaker *[1 mark]* / the level of other substances in the mineral solution *[1 mark]* / the size of the beakers *[1 mark]* / the amount of air available *[1 mark]* / the amount of water available *[1 mark]* / the temperature of the beakers *[1 mark]*.

7.5 E.g. they could carry out repeats of the experiment and calculate a mean result for each beaker *[1 mark]*.

7.6 E.g. pea plants of this species increase in height at a faster rate with both magnesium and nitrates *[1 mark]*.

8.1 The cell must grow and increase its number of subcellular structures *[1 mark]*. It must also duplicate its DNA *[1 mark]*.

8.2 Membranes will form around the two sets of chromosomes / two separate nuclei will form *[1 mark]*. The cytoplasm and cell membrane will divide *[1 mark]*.

You can see from Figure 6 that the chromosomes in cell Y have been pulled to either end of the cell. That means that the cell is ready to divide into two.

8.3 $2 \times 60 = 120$ minutes
$120 \div 20 = 6$ divisions
So number of cells $= 20 \times 2^6 = 1280 = \textbf{1.28} \times \textbf{10}^3$
[3 marks for the correct answer in standard form, otherwise 1 mark for calculating 6 divisions and 1 mark for 1280]

If you start with one cell, you need to multiply 2 by itself for the number of divisions (in this case that's 2^6). However, as you're starting with 20 cells here, the total number of cells will be 20 times greater than if you started with just one cell — so you need to multiply 2^6 by 20.

8.4 Stage: B *[1 mark]*. Reason: e.g. this stage results in the division of a single cell into many identical cells/clones, each of which has a full copy of the genetic material *[1 mark]*.

9.1 E.g. the bone marrow will contain stem cells *[1 mark]*. These will differentiate in the patient to produce new plasma cells, replacing those killed during chemotherapy *[1 mark]*.

9.2 How to grade your answer:
Level 0: There is no relevant information. *[No marks]*
Level 1: There is a brief comparison of the advantages and disadvantages of using the two types of stem cell in medical treatments, but there is no overall conclusion as to which would be the most beneficial, or there is a conclusion which is inconsistent with the reasoning provided. *[1 to 2 marks]*
Level 2: There is a clear comparison of the advantages and disadvantages of using the two types of stem cell in medical treatments. A conclusion, which is consistent with the reasoning provided, is given as to which would be most beneficial. *[3 to 4 marks]*
Here are some points your answer may include:
Adult stem cells are able to differentiate into a smaller range of cell types than embryonic stem cells, which are capable of developing into most types of cell. This means embryonic stem cells may be used to treat a wider range of conditions than adult stem cells.
Adult stem cells which come from the patient's own body are less likely to be rejected than embryonic stem cells. However, therapeutic cloning offers a way to produce embryonic stem cells that won't be rejected by the body.
There are ethical issues with using embryonic stem cells, which don't apply to using adult stem cells. For example, some people feel that human embryos shouldn't be used as a source of stem cells as each one is a potential human life.

Make sure you finish your answer with a conclusion about which type of stem cell would be most beneficial for medical treatments. Your conclusion must be supported by the line of reasoning in your answer. E.g. "overall, embryonic stem cells would be most beneficial for medical treatments — although there are more ethical issues associated with using them, they could be used to treat a wider range of conditions than adult stem cells and therapeutic cloning can be used to ensure they are not rejected by the patient's body."

10.1 Deaths in 1970 = 2500
Deaths in 2000 = 1000
2500 – 1000 = 1500 deaths
2000 – 1970 = 30 years
Rate of decrease $= 1500 \div 30 = \textbf{50 deaths per year}$ *[2 marks for correct answer, otherwise 1 mark for correct working]*

Make sure you read the axes carefully when you take information from a graph — here the y-axis gives the number of deaths in hundreds.

10.2 3000 (accept answers in the range of 2900 to 3100) *[1 mark]*

10.3 Any two from: e.g. they should have sterilised the Petri dishes/culture medium/agar before use. / They should have sterilised the inoculating loops (used to transfer the bacteria to the culture medium) by passing them through a flame. / They should have taped on the lids of the Petri dishes. / They should have stored the Petri dishes/agar plates upside down. *[2 marks — 1 mark for each correct answer]*

10.4 How to grade your answer:
Level 0: There is no relevant information. *[No marks]*
Level 1: There is a brief attempt to link a trend from Figure 8 to a piece of evidence from Figure 9. *[1 to 2 marks]*
Level 2: There is some explanation of trends from Figure 8 using evidence from Figure 9. *[3 to 4 marks]*
Level 3: There is a clear and detailed explanation of trends from Figure 8 using evidence from Figure 9. *[5 to 6 marks]*

Here are some points your answer may include:
The inhibition zones for discs 2 and 3 on the 1975 plate suggest that the antibiotic was very effective against the bacteria that cause disease X — much more effective than the control.
Having an effective antibiotic may have allowed doctors to treat disease X more effectively, therefore reducing the number of deaths from the disease between 1970 and 2000.
However, on the 2005 plate, the inhibition zone is much smaller for disc 3 and non-existent for disc 2, suggesting that the antibiotic is no longer as effective against the bacteria that cause disease X / the bacteria that cause disease X have developed resistance to this antibiotic.
A lack of an effective antibiotic may have caused death rates from disease X to increase between 2000 and 2010, as doctors would have been less able to treat the disease.

Set A — Paper 2

1.1 Two copies of the allele need to be present for the characteristic to be displayed *[1 mark]*.
1.2

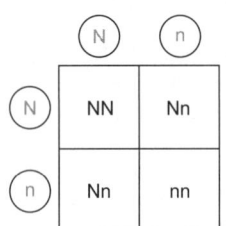

[2 marks if all the offspring's genotypes (NN, Nn, Nn and nn) are correct, otherwise 1 mark for two or three correct]

1.3 Proportion of offspring expected to have vestigial wings = 25%/0.25/1 in 4
So out of 200 fruit flies, the expected number of offspring with vestigial wings = (200 ÷ 100) × 25 / 200 × 0.25 / 200 ÷ 4 = **50**
[2 marks for the correct answer, otherwise 1 mark for the correct proportion of offspring expected to have vestigial wings]
Remember, the allele for vestigial wings is recessive, so only offspring with the genotype 'nn' will have vestigial wings.

1.4 Genetic material is stored as DNA molecules *[1 mark]*, which are arranged into chromosomes *[1 mark]*. The chromosomes are found in the nucleus of each cell *[1 mark]*.

2.1 To make sure the results were representative of the whole population in each section. / To prevent bias. *[1 mark]*

2.2 52 *[1 mark]*
Remember, the median is the middle value of a data set when the data is in numerical order.

2.3 Mean number of clover per m^2 = (87 + 96 + 88) ÷ 3 = 90.333... = **90** (2 s.f.)
[2 marks for the correct answer, otherwise 1 mark for 90.333...]

2.4 area of section C = 5 × 3 = 15 m^2
12 × 15 = **180 dandelions**
[2 marks for correct answer, otherwise 1 mark for correct working]
All you have to do here is multiply the number of dandelions found in 1 m^2 by the total area of section C.

2.5 E.g. the number of plants per m^2/density of plants/frequency of plants of all three species increases with increasing distance from the school *[1 mark]*.

2.6 Any three from: e.g. differences in temperature / differences in the mineral content of the soil / differences in the soil pH / differences in the light intensity received by the plants / differences in the moisture level of the soil / differences in the wind intensity/direction *[3 marks — 1 mark for each correct answer]*
Remember, abiotic factors are non-living parts of an ecosystem.

3.1 They contract *[1 mark]*.

3.2 Motor neurones carry electrical/nervous impulses from the central nervous system *[1 mark]* to effectors *[1 mark]*.

3.3 percentage increase = $\dfrac{\text{final value} - \text{original value}}{\text{original value}} \times 100$
$= \dfrac{0.39 - 0.30}{0.30} \times 100$
$= \mathbf{30\%}$
[2 marks for correct answer, otherwise 1 mark for correct working]

3.4

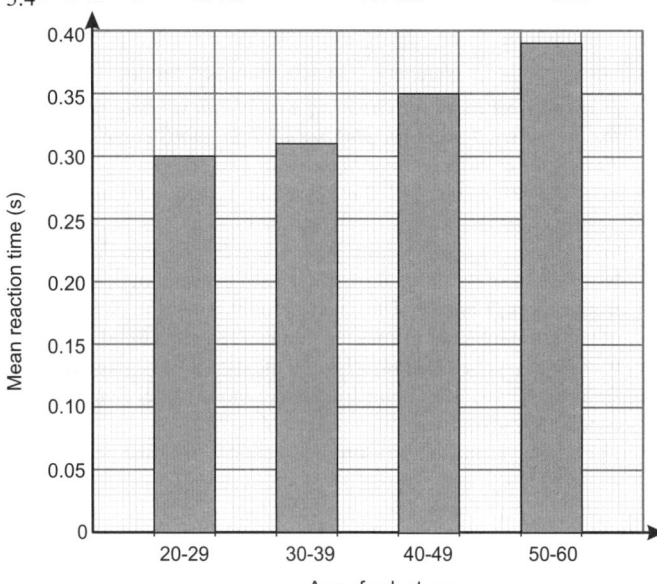

[2 marks — 1 mark for a suitable scale and label on the y-axis, 1 mark for all four bars drawn correctly.]

3.5 Any two from: e.g. they could have used volunteers with a wider range of ages. / They could have used more volunteers. / They could have used the same number of volunteers in each age group. *[2 marks — 1 mark for each correct answer]*

4.1 The medulla *[1 mark]* because this part of the brain controls unconscious activities, such as breathing *[1 mark]*.

4.2 A *[1 mark]*

4.3 Any two from: e.g. consciousness *[1 mark]* / intelligence *[1 mark]* / memory *[1 mark]* / language *[1 mark]*

4.4 E.g. the cerebellum *[1 mark]* as this is the region responsible for the muscle coordination *[1 mark]*.

4.5 Any two from: e.g. studying patients with brain damage *[1 mark]* / electrically stimulating different regions of the brain *[1 mark]* / MRI scans *[1 mark]*

5.1 phototropism *[1 mark]*

5.2 E.g. the type of plant shoots used. / The intensity of the light source. / The temperature the plants were kept at. / The medium (e.g. soil) the shoots were grown in. / The amount of water the shoots received. *[1 mark]*

5.3 How to grade your answer:
  Level 0: There is no relevant information. *[No marks]*
  Level 1: There are some relevant points explaining the growth of one or both shoots, but the answer is lacking in detail. *[1 to 2 marks]*
  Level 2: There is a clear, detailed explanation of the students' results for both shoot A and shoot B. *[3 to 4 marks]*
  Here are some points your answer may include:
  Auxin is produced in the tips of plant shoots.
  In shoot A, more auxin has accumulated on the side of the shoot tip that is in the shade.
  This has caused the cells on the shaded side of the shoot to elongate faster than those nearest the light, so the shoot has grown towards the light.
  In shoot B, the tip is not exposed to light so auxin is equally distributed on both sides of the shoot.
  This means the cells on both sides have elongated at the same rate, causing the shoot to grow straight up.

5.4 The root has grown downwards, towards gravity / the shoot has changed the direction of its growth due to gravity / the shoot has exhibited geotropism/gravitropism *[1 mark]*. This is because gravity has caused more auxin to accumulate on the lower side of the root *[1 mark]*. Auxin inhibits growth in root cells *[1 mark]*, so cells on the top of the root have elongated faster than those on the bottom *[1 mark]*.

5.5 It is used in rooting powder, which causes cuttings to quickly grow roots *[1 mark]*.

5.6 It can be used to control seed dormancy *[1 mark]*, induce flowering / grow bigger flowers *[1 mark]* and grow larger fruit *[1 mark]*.

5.7 E.g. unripe fruit is exposed to ethene while it is being transported *[1 mark]*. The ethene stimulates enzymes in the fruit that cause it to ripen, so the fruit will be ripe by the time it reaches the customer *[1 mark]*.

6.1 Each gene contains a sequence of bases *[1 mark]*. The order of bases in a gene determines the order of amino acids in a protein *[1 mark]*.

6.2 E.g. the herbicide-resistance gene could have been cut out of the other plant species using enzymes *[1 mark]*. The gene could have then been inserted into a vector (e.g. a virus/bacterial plasmid) *[1 mark]*. The vector would then have been used to insert the genes into the cells of the crop plant *[1 mark]*.

6.3 They're used as a control *[1 mark]* to show how grass plants that could not have been affected by the GM crop respond to spraying *[1 mark]*.

6.4 E.g. they could repeat the experiment using a different method/ equipment / ask other scientists to repeat their experiment and check the results are similar *[1 mark]*.

6.5 Agree, because a difference of two plants out of 100 could just be due to chance *[1 mark]*.

6.6 No. Just because the genes did not spread in this experiment, does not mean that they won't in the future/at other sites *[1 mark]*. A lot more evidence would need to be gathered/the experiment would need to be reproduced before you could be reasonably certain that the GM crop posed no threat *[1 mark]*.

7.1 Both producers use energy from non-living sources to increase their biomass/provide food for other organisms in a food web *[1 mark]*. However, the bacteria use chemicals in the hydrothermal vent to do this, whereas plants use energy from the Sun *[1 mark]*.

7.2 extremophiles *[1 mark]*

7.3 E.g. they will have enzymes that have high optimum temperatures *[1 mark]*. This will mean that the enzymes don't denature/will still function at high temperatures *[1 mark]*.

7.4 How to grade your answer:
  Level 0: There is no relevant information. *[No marks]*
  Level 1: There are some relevant points explaining how the population sizes of some of the organisms in the food web may be affected but the answer is missing some detail. *[1 to 2 marks]*
  Level 2: There is a clear, detailed explanation of how the population sizes of all of the organisms in the food web may be affected. *[3 to 4 marks]*
  Here are some points your answer may include:
  The population of crabs might decrease in size, as there would be fewer tubeworms for them to eat.
  Fewer crabs could then cause the population of octopuses to decrease in size as they would have less food to eat.
  The population of bacteria might increase as there would be fewer tubeworms to eat them.
  If so, the population size of the shrimps might rise, as there would be more bacteria for them to eat.
  More shrimps might lead to an increase in the population size of fish, as they would have more food to eat.
  In turn, more fish could lead to a rise in the population size of octopuses as they would also have more food to eat.
  This could counteract any fall in the population size of octopuses caused by the fall in crab numbers.

8.1 Point at which ADH is most likely to be released: B *[1 mark]*
  Explanation: this is where the water content of the blood is lowest *[1 mark]*. ADH is released when the water content of the blood is too low, so the kidneys reabsorb more water/to increase the water content of the blood *[1 mark]*.

8.2 pituitary gland *[1 mark]*

8.3 It will cause more concentrated urine to be produced *[1 mark]*.

8.4 E.g. the person may not have taken in enough water through food/drink *[1 mark]*. The person may have been sweating a lot *[1 mark]*.

8.5 If the water content of the blood is not controlled, too much or too little water could be drawn into cells by osmosis *[1 mark]*. This could damage cells/stop them from functioning normally *[1 mark]*.

9.1 The nucleus was removed from an unfertilised sheep's egg cell *[1 mark]*. A nucleus taken from an adult body cell of another sheep was then inserted into the egg cell *[1 mark]*. The egg cell was then stimulated to divide to form an embryo by being given an electric shock *[1 mark]*. The embryo was then implanted into the womb of an adult female sheep *[1 mark]*, where it developed into Dolly — a clone of the original adult body cell *[1 mark]*.

9.2 E.g. cloning animals could mean that farmers could increase the amount of food they produced faster than using traditional methods of breeding *[1 mark]*. However, cloning could lead to a population of animals that have little resistance to certain diseases *[1 mark]*. Cloning could also lead to health problems in the animals *[1 mark]*. Overall, the use of cloning in agriculture could enable more food to be produced more quickly, but traditional methods of breeding are better as they raise fewer ethical concerns *[1 mark]*.

There are other things you could have written about here, but it's important that you have considered both the advantages and disadvantages of cloning before coming to a justified conclusion.

10.1 E.g. many early forms of life were soft-bodied/will have decayed before forming fossils *[1 mark]*. Early fossils may have been destroyed by geological activity *[1 mark]*.

10.2 E.g. the teeth won't have decayed easily, so they'll have lasted a long time when buried *[1 mark]*. As the teeth did decay, they will have been gradually replaced by minerals, forming a rock-like substance (the fossil) shaped like the original teeth *[1 mark]*.

10.3 How to grade your answer:
Level 0: There is no relevant information. *[No marks]*
Level 1: A brief outline of how chimpanzees and bonobos have evolved from the same common ancestor is given. *[1 to 2 marks]*
Level 2: Some explanation of how chimpanzees and bonobos have evolved from the same common ancestor is given, with reference to genetic variation, natural selection or speciation. *[3 to 4 marks]*
Level 3: A clear, full and detailed explanation of how chimpanzees and bonobos evolved from the same common ancestor, with reference to genetic variation, natural selection and speciation. *[5 to 6 marks]*

Here are some points your answer may include:
The isolated populations on either side of the river showed genetic variation because they had a wide range of alleles.
In each population, individuals with characteristics that made them better adapted to their environment were more likely to survive and breed successfully.
The alleles that controlled the beneficial characteristics were more likely to get passed on to the next generation.
Conditions to the north and south of the river may have been slightly different, so the features that were beneficial may have been different for each population.
Because of this, different characteristics will have become more common in each population due to natural selection.
Eventually, individuals in the populations to the north and south of the river may have developed such different features that they were no longer able to interbreed to produce fertile offspring.
They became the new species of chimpanzees and bonobos.

Set B — Paper 1

1.1 cell wall *[1 mark]*
1.2 A — Carrying out photosynthesis.
B — Controlling the movement of gases in and out of the plant.
C — Carrying water and ions around the plant.
[2 marks for all 3 correct, otherwise 1 mark for 1 correct]
1.3 Meristem tissue contains stem cells *[1 mark]*, which can differentiate into any type of cell *[1 mark]*.
1.4 A root hair cell has a long extension *[1 mark]*, which gives the cell a large surface area *[1 mark]*. This allows the cell to absorb more water and mineral ions into the plant *[1 mark]*.
1.5 $C_6H_{12}O_6$ *[1 mark]*
1.6 It contains the genetic material which controls the activities of the cell *[1 mark]*.
1.7 E.g. animal cells don't have a cell wall. Animal cells don't contain chloroplasts. Animal cells don't have a permanent vacuole. *[3 marks — 1 mark for each correct answer.]*
2.1 Alexander Fleming *[1 mark]*
2.2 9 days *[1 mark]*
2.3 Different antibiotics kill different types of bacteria, so it's important that the patient is treated with the right one *[1 mark]*.
2.4 Viruses reproduce using human body cells *[1 mark]* so it is difficult to develop drugs that destroy the virus without killing the body's cells *[1 mark]*.
2.5 phagocytosis *[1 mark]*
2.6 They produce antibodies *[1 mark]*. They produce antitoxins *[1 mark]*.
2.7 size of real object = size of image ÷ magnification
So, actual length of bacterium = 3 mm ÷ 600 = **0.005 mm**
[2 marks for correct answer, otherwise 1 mark for correct working]

3.1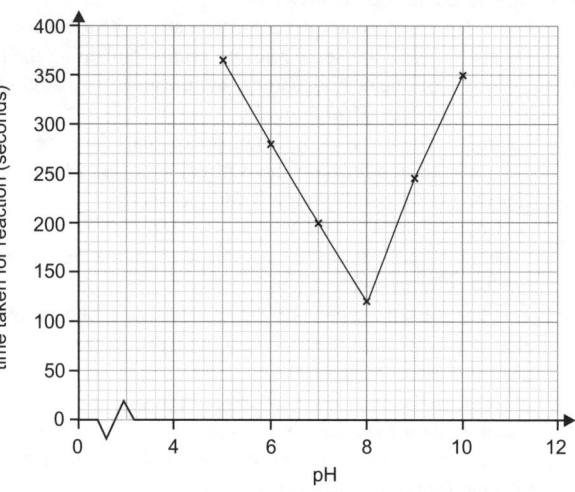

[4 marks — 1 mark for labelling the y-axis correctly and using a suitable scale, 2 marks for all points correctly plotted or 1 mark for 5 points correctly plotted, 1 mark for joining the points with a smooth curve.]
3.2 pH 8 *[1 mark]*
The optimum pH is the pH at which the reaction happens fastest.
3.3 Dependent variable: time taken for reaction *[1 mark]*
Independent variable: pH *[1 mark]*
3.4 E.g. high and low pH values may have caused bonds holding the enzyme's structure together to break *[1 mark]*. This may have changed the shape of the enzyme's active site/denatured the enzyme *[1 mark]*, meaning that it could no longer speed up the reaction *[1 mark]*.
3.5 It would have allowed her to control the temperature of the solutions *[1 mark]* so that she could be sure that small variations in temperature wouldn't affect her results *[1 mark]*.
3.6 Colour: purple *[1 mark]*
Reason: because the presence of trypsin will give a positive result to the biuret test *[1 mark]*.
Remember, biuret solution tests for the presence of proteins. The trypsin won't have been used up in the reaction, so it will still cause a positive result, even at the end of the experiment.
4.1 E.g. capillaries are very small *[1 mark]*, which means that they can carry blood very close to the alveoli *[1 mark]*. / Capillaries have very thin walls *[1 mark]*, which reduces the distances over which gases have to diffuse *[1 mark]*. / Capillaries have permeable walls *[1 mark]*, which allows gases to diffuse across them *[1 mark]*.
4.2 Cells produce carbon dioxide during respiration *[1 mark]*, which gets carried in the blood to the lungs where it is breathed out *[1 mark]*.
4.3 The trachea is lined with cells that have cilia *[1 mark]* and cells that secrete mucus *[1 mark]*, meaning that pathogens entering the trachea are trapped and moved back up to the throat to be swallowed *[1 mark]*. If these cells are damaged then pathogens will be more likely to enter the lungs and cause infections *[1 mark]*.
4.4 How to grade your answer:
Level 0: There is no relevant information. *[No marks]*
Level 1: There is a brief explanation of why people who smoke may need to breathe more quickly when exercising than non-smokers. *[1 to 2 marks]*
Level 2: There is a detailed explanation of why people who smoke may need to breathe more quickly when exercising than non-smokers. *[3 to 4 marks]*
Here are some points your answer may include:
During exercise, muscles need more energy in order to contract.
This means that the rate of respiration increases in order to release the extra energy.
An increased rate of respiration means that more oxygen is needed in cells.

Oxygen diffuses into the blood from air that is breathed into the lungs, across the walls of the alveoli.

Since smoking can reduce the surface area of the alveoli, this will reduce the rate of diffusion of oxygen into the blood. This means that less oxygen will move into the blood after each breath.

So, when smokers exercise, they may need to breathe faster than non-smokers in order to deliver enough oxygen to their cells to meet the increased rate of respiration.

5.1 Tube A *[1 mark]*. The solution has gone brick-red after being tested with Benedict's reagent, so this tube contains the most reducing sugar *[1 mark]*. This means the rate of digestion was quickest with this concentration of amylase *[1 mark]*.

5.2 The reducing sugars diffused from the solution inside the Visking tubing to the water surrounding it *[1 mark]*, because the concentration of reducing sugars was greater in the Visking tubing than in the water *[1 mark]*.

5.3 The surface area would have affected how fast the sugars moved out into the surrounding solution *[1 mark]*. If the rate of movement was different between the test tubes, then this would have affected the test results *[1 mark]*.

5.4 E.g. he didn't start the stop clock until all the lengths of Visking tubing had been placed in the test tubes *[1 mark]*, meaning that some of the solutions were left to react for longer than others *[1 mark]*. / He used the same pipette to add different concentrations of amylase to the tubing *[1 mark]*, which may have lead to some solutions being contaminated with a solution of a different concentration *[1 mark]*. / He didn't measure out equal volumes of amylase and starch solution for each length of tubing *[1 mark]*, meaning that some lengths of tubing may have had more or less enzyme and substrate than others *[1 mark]*.

5.5 Any two from: e.g. salivary glands / pancreas / small intestine *[2 marks — 1 mark for each correct answer.]*

5.6 Starch is large and insoluble *[1 mark]* and therefore cannot be absorbed through the walls of the digestive system *[1 mark]*, whereas small, soluble sugars can be absorbed *[1 mark]*.

6.1 How to grade your answer:
Level 0: There is no relevant information. *[No marks]*
Level 1: There is a brief explanation of how the HPV vaccine may help to protect a woman against cervical cancer. *[1 to 2 marks]*
Level 2: There is a detailed explanation of how the HPV vaccine may help to protect a woman against cervical cancer. *[3 to 4 marks]*
Here are some points your answer may include:
The vaccine may contain small amounts of inactive HPV.
This will be injected into the woman's bloodstream.
The HPV particles carry antigens which will cause the woman's immune system to react by producing antibodies. The antibodies will attack the HPV particles.
Then, if the woman is ever infected with an active version of one of the same strains of the virus as in the vaccine, her immune system will be able to respond more rapidly to the infection and will be able to get rid of the pathogen more quickly.
This will mean that the virus will be less likely to cause cervical cancer in the woman.

6.2 If a large percentage of the population are vaccinated against the HPV virus, then that proportion of the population will be better able to defend themselves against the virus *[1 mark]*. This will mean that there will be fewer people who can pass on the virus *[1 mark]*.

6.3 Proportion of sexually active young women with HPV infection in 2008 = 17.6%
So number of sexually active young women expected to have HPV infection from a sample of 2000 = 17.6% of 2000
= (2000 ÷ 100) × 17.6 = **352**
[2 marks for the correct answer, otherwise 1 mark for reading 17.6% from the graph.]

6.4 E.g. the vaccination programme was quite expensive since it cost £18.9 million for the NHS to implement it in 2008/09 *[1 mark]*. The vaccine can also sometimes cause negative side effects, including soreness at the site of injection and difficulty breathing *[1 mark]*. However, overall the programme was beneficial *[1 mark]* since it was effective in reducing the proportion of sexually active young women between the ages of 16 and 18 infected with HPV *[1 mark]*.

You could also have said that the more serious side effects only occurred in very rare cases and therefore that the vaccine was not dangerous to most of the young women who had it. You could have also mentioned that if fewer women are infected with HPV it's likely that fewer women will get cervical cancer.

6.5 Any two from: e.g. smoking / ionising radiation / faulty genes *[2 marks — 1 mark for each correct answer]*

7.1 radius (r) = diameter ÷ 2 = 12.0 ÷ 2 = 6.0 mm
area = $\pi(6.0^2) = \pi \times 36 = 113.09... = $ **113 mm²** (to 3 s.f.)
[2 marks for the correct answer, otherwise 1 mark for $\pi \times 36$]

It doesn't matter whether you used the π button on your calculator or 3.14 instead — your final answer should still be the same.

7.2 4 × 60 = 240 minutes
Number of divisions = 240 ÷ 24 = 10
Number of bacterial cells = $2^{10} = $ **1024**
[2 marks for the correct answer, otherwise 1 mark for correctly calculating 10 divisions]

7.3 To kill microorganisms on the loop / to sterilise the loop *[1 mark]* and therefore prevent unwanted microorganisms from contaminating the agar plate and affecting the results *[1 mark]*.

7.4 Any two from: e.g. she should have kept the Bunsen burner on a heat-proof mat *[1 mark]*. / She should have made sure that the flame was yellow and visible when it was not heating anything *[1 mark]*. / She should have made sure that there was nothing flammable near the Bunsen burner *[1 mark]*.

7.5 The scientist will measure the clear areas around each of the paper discs on the plate *[1 mark]*. The paper disc with the largest clear area will contain the most effective disinfectant *[1 mark]*.

8.1 At low temperatures the rate of photosynthesis is low because the enzymes needed for photosynthesis are working slowly *[1 mark]*. As temperature increases, the enzymes work faster, so the graph goes up in a straight line *[1 mark]*. The rate of photosynthesis is highest where the graph peaks, because this is the optimum temperature for the enzymes/the temperature at which the enzymes work best *[1 mark]*. After this, the rate of photosynthesis falls rapidly as the enzymes change shape/are denatured *[1 mark]*.

8.2 E.g.

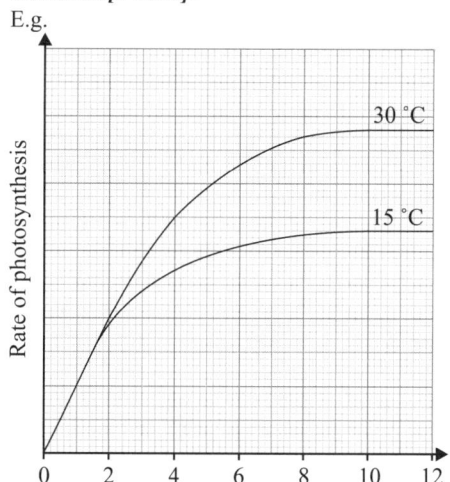

[1 mark for drawing a line that rises at the same rate as the line for 30 °C at first, plus 1 mark for drawing the line levelling off at a lower rate of photosynthesis than the line for 30 °C]

8.3 The light intensity will be four times greater than it was before. *[1 mark]*

8.4 How to grade your answer:

Level 0: There is no relevant information. *[No marks]*

Level 1: A brief outline is given of one or two advantages or disadvantages to the farmer of growing his plants in the conditions within the greenhouse, but there is no overall conclusion or the conclusion given is inconsistent with the reasoning provided. *[1 to 2 marks]*

Level 2: There is a clear explanation of several advantages and disadvantages to the farmer of growing his plants in the conditions within the greenhouse. A conclusion is given that is consistent with the reasoning provided. *[3 to 4 marks]*

Level 3: There is a clear, full and detailed explanation of the advantages and disadvantages to the farmer of growing his plants in the conditions within the greenhouse. There is a conclusion which is fully supported by the reasoning provided. *[5 to 6 marks]*

Here are some points your answer may include:

Using lamps in the greenhouse on winter evenings will mean that the plants will photosynthesise for longer than if they were kept outside.

This will mean that the farmer will be able to grow more / bigger plants and may mean that the farmer will be able to earn more money from the plants. However, the £25 monthly cost from keeping the plants in these light conditions may not be covered by this increase in the number / size of plants.

Furthermore, a light intensity of 11 arbitrary units will result in the same rate of photosynthesis as a light intensity of at least 9.6 arbitrary units according to Figure 9, therefore it may waste the farmer's money to have the light intensity kept at this higher level.

30 °C is near the optimum temperature for photosynthesis in the plants according to Figure 8.

It is also significantly warmer than the average outside temperature of 4 °C during the winter months.

Therefore keeping the temperature at this level is likely to mean that the farmer's plants will grow at an increased rate and may result in more / bigger plants for the farmer.

However, it will be expensive for the farmer to maintain the heat at this level since it costs £140 a month and the increase in number / size of plants may not cover this additional cost.

Furthermore, a slightly lower temperature may result in a similar rate of photosynthesis according to Figure 8 and would also be less expensive to maintain.

Overall it might be better for the farmer to grow his plants outside rather than in the conditions he's chosen for his greenhouse. The costs associated with the heating and lighting might not outweigh the benefits of a higher rate of photosynthesis. However, it is possible that it would be beneficial for the farmer to keep his plants in the greenhouse using less energy-consuming levels of temperature and lighting.

It doesn't matter whether you conclude that it would be more advantageous for the farmer to grow his plants outside or in the greenhouse, as long as the reasoning in your answer supports the conclusion that you give.

Set B — Paper 2

1.1 23 *[1 mark]*

1.2 The entire set of genetic material in an organism *[1 mark]*.

1.3 Males have one X chromosome and one Y chromosome *[1 mark]*. Females have two X chromosomes *[1 mark]*.

1.4 meiosis *[1 mark]*

1.5 The new cell divides by mitosis *[1 mark]*. The two new cells continue to divide to create lots of new cells in the embryo *[1 mark]*. As the embryo develops, the cells differentiate into the specialised cells that make the organism *[1 mark]*.

2.1 pancreas *[1 mark]*

2.2 260 000 ÷ 16 = **16 250 people** *[1 mark]*

2.3 E.g. unhealthy diets can lead to obesity, which is a risk factor for Type 2 diabetes *[1 mark]*.

2.4 E.g. by eating a carbohydrate-controlled diet *[1 mark]* and by getting regular exercise *[1 mark]*.

2.5 He needs to inject insulin to lower his blood glucose level *[1 mark]* because his pancreas doesn't produce enough insulin/ produces no insulin *[1 mark]*.

2.6 12:30 *[1 mark]*

After 12:30 there is a sharp decrease in the blood glucose level because the injection of insulin is causing glucose to move into the body cells.

3.1 E.g. they don't shed much hair *[1 mark]*.

3.2 Initially Labrador retrievers with a gentle temperament could be bred with poodles that don't shed much hair/don't cause a reaction in people with dog allergies *[1 mark]*. From the offspring, dogs with the most gentle temperaments and that shed the least hair/cause the least reaction in people with dog allergies could be bred together *[1 mark]*. This process could be repeated over many generations until dogs with a gentle temperament and that are suitable for people with dog allergies are consistently created *[1 mark]*.

3.3 E.g. selective breeding can lead to inbreeding, which can cause an increased chance of organisms inheriting harmful genetic defects *[1 mark]*. Inbreeding can also lead to a population being wiped out by a new disease *[1 mark]*.

4.1 Any three from: e.g. the birth rate of many developing countries is rising quickly. / As diets in developed countries change, more food is transported out of developing countries, making the food resources there more scarce. / Farming can be affected by new pests and pathogens which can result in the loss of crops and livestock. / Changes in the environmental conditions (e.g. a lack of rain) can result in the loss of crops and livestock, and can lead to widespread famine. / In some areas, the high input costs of farming can make it too expensive for people to start or maintain food production, leading to a lack of food in these areas. / In some parts of the world, there are conflicts that affect the availability of food and water. *[3 marks — 1 for each correct answer]*

4.2 C *[1 mark]*. This is the shortest food chain. As energy is lost at each stage/trophic level in a food chain, the shortest chain will be most efficient *[1 mark]*.

4.3 efficiency = $\dfrac{700}{8000} \times 100$ = **8.75%** *[1 mark]*

4.4 C *[1 mark]*, because at this farm the birds have the least space available, so they will have the most limited movement *[1 mark]* and they are kept in the warmest environment so they will lose the least heat *[1 mark]*. Restricting movement and heat loss saves energy, so the transfer of energy from the feed to the turkeys is more efficient *[1 mark]*.

5.1 Each new plant inherited one allele for round seed coats and one allele for wrinkled seed coats *[1 mark]*. Since all the offspring had round seed coats, this allele must be dominant *[1 mark]*.

5.2 E.g.

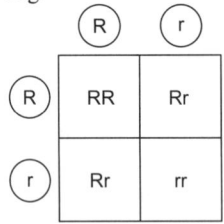

Phenotype of each offspring: RR and Rr = round, rr = wrinkled. *[3 marks — 1 mark for gametes' genotypes correct, 1 mark for offsprings' genotypes correct, 1 mark for correctly identifying offsprings' phenotypes.]*

5.3 5474 ÷ 1850 = 2.96 (to 3 s.f.), so the ratio is **2.96 : 1** *[1 mark]*

5.4 E.g. because scientists in Mendel's time had no knowledge of genes or DNA, so they did not understand the significance of his work *[1 mark]*.

6.1

	percentage increase in mass (%)		
Block number	Stem tissue	Leaf tissue	Root tissue
1	119	33	76
2	97	21	62
3	100	17	58
4	114	25	(192)
5	125	39	92
Mean	**X**	27	72

[1 mark]

6.2 $(119 + 97 + 100 + 114 + 125) \div 5 = $ **111** *[1 mark]*

6.3 E.g.

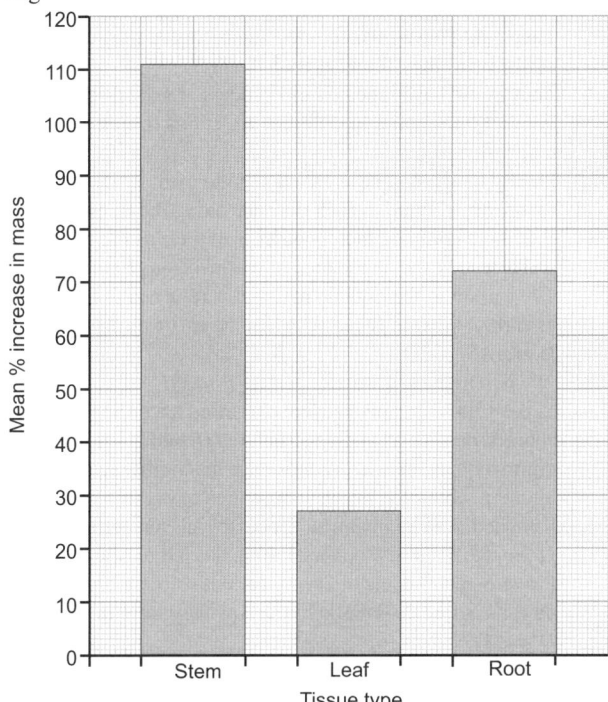

[2 marks — 1 mark for two correct axes, including a correct scale on the y-axis, 1 mark for all three bars plotted correctly. Allow the plotting mark if incorrect answer to 6.2 has been correctly plotted.]

6.4 % increase in mass of root tissue grown in growth medium 1 = 72%
So % increase in mass of root tissue grown in growth medium 4 = 72 × 2.5 = **180%** *[1 mark]*

6.5 The mass of the plant tissue *[1 mark]*.

6.6 E.g. the temperature / the size of the tissue samples/blocks / the volume of the growth medium / the time that the blocks were left incubating *[1 mark]*.

6.7 E.g. to prevent contamination by microorganisms *[1 mark]*.

6.8 E.g. reading the mass from a mass balance is likely to be more precise than measuring length using a ruler / the resolution of a mass balance is greater than that of a ruler / measuring length using a ruler only takes into account growth in one dimension, whereas measuring mass takes into account growth of the whole block *[1 mark]*.

6.9 The scientists could have grown blocks of stem, leaf and root tissue on a growth medium that didn't contain any plant growth hormone *[1 mark]* but kept all other variables (e.g. other components of the growth medium) the same *[1 mark]*.

7.1 E.g. there is an increasing level of methane / carbon dioxide *[1 mark]*.

7.2 As the average April temperature increases, the first day that the swallow is seen in Britain gets earlier *[1 mark]*.

7.3 Valid data is repeatable, reproducible and answers the original question *[1 mark]*. There is evidence to suggest that the results of both studies are likely to be reproducible as they were both conducted over long time periods / both studies found similar results *[1 mark]*. However, more information would be needed about other factors that may be affecting the swallows' migration patterns to prove that global warming is causing the changes seen *[1 mark]*, so the data doesn't answer the original question *[1 mark]*.

8.1 How to grade your answer:
Level 0: There is no relevant information. *[No marks]*
Level 1: There is a brief outline of how hormones interact to control the menstrual cycle. The answer mentions two hormones from FSH, oestrogen, LH or progesterone. *[1 to 2 marks]*
Level 2: Some explanation of how hormones interact to control the menstrual cycle is given. The answer mentions three hormones from FSH, oestrogen, LH or progesterone. *[3 to 4 marks]*
Level 3: A clear, full and detailed explanation of how hormones interact to control the menstrual cycle is given. The answer refers to FSH, oestrogen, LH and progesterone. *[5 to 6 marks]*

Here are some points your answer may include:
FSH/follicle stimulating hormone causes an egg to mature in a follicle in one of the ovaries.
It also stimulates the ovaries to produce oestrogen.
Oestrogen causes the lining of the uterus to grow.
It also inhibits the further release of FSH and stimulates the release of LH/luteinising hormone.
LH stimulates the release of an egg from the ovary around the middle of the menstrual cycle.
After egg release, the empty follicle starts to produce progesterone.
Progesterone maintains the lining during the second half of the menstrual cycle.
Progesterone also inhibits the release of FSH and LH.
When the level of progesterone falls, the uterus lining breaks down and the cycle starts again.

8.2 FSH and LH are given to a woman to stimulate several eggs to mature *[1 mark]*. Eggs are then collected from her ovaries and fertilised in a lab using a man's sperm *[1 mark]*. These are then grown into embryos *[1 mark]*. Once the embryos are tiny balls of cells, one or two of them are transferred to the woman's uterus/womb *[1 mark]*.

8.3 Any two from: e.g. it can be emotionally and physically stressful. / The success rates of fertility treatments are low. / There is an increased chance of having multiple births, which can be risky for the mother and babies. *[2 marks — 1 mark for each correct answer]*

9.1 E.g.

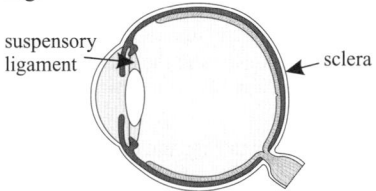

[2 marks — 1 for each correct label]

9.2 The iris contains muscles *[1 mark]*, which allow it to control the diameter of the pupil and therefore the amount of light entering the eye *[1 mark]*.

9.3 The ciliary muscles relax *[1 mark]*, which allows the suspensory ligaments to pull tight *[1 mark]*. This makes the lens go thin *[1 mark]*, so it refracts light by a smaller amount *[1 mark]*.

9.4

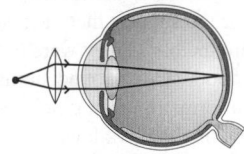

[1 mark for a convex lens (a lens that curves outwards),
1 mark for light rays correctly focused on the retina]

9.5 Any two from: e.g. fewer general NHS sight tests were carried out in England and Wales in 2014-2015 than 2013-2014 *[1 mark]*. / The overall decrease in the number of general NHS sight tests between 2013-2014 and 2014-2015 was greater for Wales than it was for England *[1 mark]*. / More general NHS sight tests were carried out for children in England in 2014-2015 than in 2013-2014 *[1 mark]*. / Fewer general NHS sight tests were carried out in England for people aged 60+ in 2014-2015 than 2013-2014 *[1 mark]*.

9.6 E.g.
Number of sight tests in 2014-2015 = 5.5 million
Number of sight tests in 2013-2014 = 5.5 + 0.1 = 5.6 million

$$\text{percentage decrease} = \frac{\text{decrease}}{\text{original value}} \times 100$$

$$= \frac{100\ 000}{5\ 600\ 000} \times 100$$

$$= 1.7857... = \textbf{1.8\%}\ (2\ \text{s.f.})$$

[3 marks for correct answer to 2 s.f., otherwise 1 mark for
5.6 million and 1 mark for 1.7857...]

10.1 They should have worked out the mean number of organisms per m² *[1 mark]* and then multiplied this number by the total area (in m²) of the reservoir bed *[1 mark]*.

10.2 E.g. they could have used more quadrats. / They could have dug deeper at each quadrat. / They could have used bigger quadrats. *[1 mark]*

10.3 E.g. by returning the worms to the reservoir bed at the end of the investigation / by handling the worms humanely *[1 mark]*.

10.4 E.g. they may have miscounted the worms in each sample. / They may have incorrectly measured the depth that they dug to at each quadrat. / Trampling on the reservoir bed while collecting the data may have disturbed the earthworms and caused them to move towards/away from the quadrats. *[1 mark]*

10.5 How to grade your answer:
Level 0: There is no relevant information. *[No marks]*
Level 1: A brief description of a suitable method is given but the answer is lacking in detail. *[1 to 2 marks]*
Level 2: A thorough description of a suitable method is given. *[3 to 4 marks]*
Here are some points your answer may include:
The scientists could have used a tape measure to mark out a transect line from the centre of the reservoir bed to the outer scrubland.
They could have placed quadrats at regular intervals along the transect line.
At each quadrat, they could have dug down to a set depth/0.3 m and collected the soil they removed.
They could have then counted and recorded the number of earthworms they found at each quadrat.
They could have repeated this process at least three times using transect lines going in different directions from the centre of the reservoir bed.
Finally they could have calculated the mean number of earthworms found at each distance along the transect lines.

10.6 E.g. there could be factors other than the organic content of the soil affecting the abundance of earthworms *[1 mark]*.

10.7 The carbon in the organic material is returned to the atmosphere as carbon dioxide *[1 mark]* when the earthworms respire *[1 mark]*.

10.8 The common earthworm's genus *[1 mark]*.

10.9 In the 1700s, organisms were classified according to their characteristics and visible structures *[1 mark]*. However, improvements in microscopes have meant that scientists can find out more about the internal structures of organisms *[1 mark]*. Knowledge of biochemical processes has also progressed *[1 mark]*. This new understanding has led to scientists putting forward new models of classification, so some organisms are now classified differently to the way they were in the 1700s *[1 mark]*.

Acknowledgements

Graph showing prevalence of HPV on page 14 of Set B, Paper 1 © Crown copyright 2015. Reproduced under the terms of the Open Government Licence v3.0. http://www.nationalarchives.gov.uk/doc/open-government-licence/version/3/

Data used to construct the graph on page 14 of Set B, Paper 2 from International Journal of Biometeorology February 1999, Volume 42, Issue 3, pp 134-138. Phenology and the changing pattern of bird migration in Britain by T. H. Sparks. Used with permission from Springer: www.springer.com.

Data on general NHS sight tests in England on page 20 of Set B, Paper 2 from the Optical Sector Report 2014-15. Copyright © 2016. Reused with the permission of the Health and Social Care Information Centre, also known as NHS Digital. All rights reserved. Licenced under the terms of the Open Government Licence v3.0 http://www.nationalarchives.gov.uk/doc/open-government-licence/version/3/

Data on general NHS sight tests in Wales on page 20 of Set B, Paper 2 reproduced under the terms of the Open Government Licence v3.0. http://www.nationalarchives.gov.uk/doc/open-government-licence/version/3/

Every effort has been made to locate copyright holders and obtain permission to reproduce sources. For those sources where it has been difficult to trace the originator of the work, we would be grateful for information. If any copyright holder would like us to make an amendment to the acknowledgements, please notify us and we will gladly update the book at the next reprint. Thank you.